PRAISE FOR PATRICK BROWN AND *BUTTERFLY MIND*

"*Butterfly Mind* is a compelling account of Patrick Brown's three decades as an intrepid reporter for CBC radio and television. . . . Intelligence and moral outrage inform the lean prose. . . . The reportage, too, is excellent." — *Globe and Mail*

"A striking study of the eerie parallels between struggles with alcohol and autocrats . . . an incisive analysis of the major political convulsions of the past three decades . . . As [Brown] stumbles toward honesty, openness, and eventual recovery in his personal life, hope mounts that his political characters can do the same."
— *The Walrus*

". . . fascinating . . . Brown's personal story distinguishes *Butterfly Mind* from other I-was-there journalistic memoirs."
— *Montreal Gazette*

". . . engaging reportage, marked by affection and curiosity, tinged with grace." — *Winnipeg Free Press*

"A witty and trenchant chronicle of Brown's travels around the globe, covering the rise and fall of despots, the downfall of communism in Eastern Europe, and the disastrous policies of the United Nations in places like East Timor." — *Toronto Star*

"A fascinating read . . . Brown's international perspective may be unparalleled among Canadian journalists of his generation."
— *Quill & Quire*

"Interesting and engaging." — *Vue Weekly*

BUTTERFLY MIND

Revolution, Recovery, and One Reporter's
Road to Understanding China

PATRICK BROWN

ANANSI

First published in hardcover in 2008 by House of Anansi Press Inc.

This edition published in 2009 by
House of Anansi Press Inc.
110 Spadina Avenue, Suite 801
Toronto, ON, M5V 2K4
Tel. 416-363-4343
Fax 416-363-1017
www.anansi.ca

Distributed in Canada by
HarperCollins Canada Ltd.
1995 Markham Road
Scarborough, ON, M1V 5M8
Toll free tel. 1-800-387-0117

Distributed in the United States by
Publishers Group West
1700 Fourth Street
Berkeley, CA 94710
Toll free tel. 1-800-788-3123

House of Anansi Press is committed to protecting our natural environment.
As part of our efforts, this book is printed on paper that contains
100% post-consumer recycled fibres, is acid-free, and is processed chlorine-free.

13 12 11 10 09   1 2 3 4 5

Library and Archives Canada Cataloguing in Publication

Brown, Patrick, 1947–
Butterfly mind : revolution, recovery, and one reporter's
road to understanding China / Patrick Brown.

ISBN 978-0-88784-830-8

1. Brown, Patrick, 1947– . 2. Foreign correspondents — Canada — Biography.
3. Foreign correspondents — China — Biography. 4. Foreign correspondents —
Biography. 5. Journalists — Canada — Biography. 6. Journalists — Biography.
7. Alcoholics — Biography. I. Title.

PN4913.B76A3 2009   070.4'332092   C2009-902830-1

Library of Congress Control Number: 2009929240

Cover design: Paul Hodgson
Text design and typesetting: Laura Brady, Brady Typesetting & Design

Canada Council
for the Arts

Conseil des Arts
du Canada

ONTARIO ARTS COUNCIL
CONSEIL DES ARTS DE L'ONTARIO

*We acknowledge for their financial support of our publishing program the Canada Council
for the Arts, the Ontario Arts Council, and the Government of Canada through the
Book Publishing Industry Development Program (BPIDP).*

Printed and bound in Canada

To Jesse and Dominique,
with love and admiration

CONTENTS

PROLOGUE

My mother and father's first Parents' Day at King Edward's School, Birmingham, in 1958 was a grand occasion requiring new clothes and an early start. They were proud beyond words that I had won a place at the city's best secondary school. At the end of my first term, they anticipated long, intimate chats with my teachers about the outstanding progress their remarkable child was making.

Arriving a little late despite the early start, and finding clusters of parents already waiting to speak to the teachers, my mother and father joined the nearest queue, which was for an elderly history master with a hearing aid the size of a short-wave radio and a habit of leaving the classroom in the middle of a lesson to wander the corridors humming to himself. A little intimidated by their surroundings, my parents gazed up at the ancient hammer-beam ceiling of the oak-panelled hall, dreaming of the possibilities available to me from an education they'd never had.

Their turn come at last, they introduced themselves, and had their prideful balloon burst.

"We're Patrick Brown's parents," they said.

The master paused for reflection and effect, then barked three words before turning to the next set of parents in line: "Brown! Butterfly mind!"

This disparaging dismissal became a family joke, and my father used to tease me about it often. Eventually, I came to see it as an astute unintended compliment, and I considered myself to be in good company when, years later, I first came across the Chinese classic, *Zhuangzi*.

Zhuangzi is named after its main author, Zhuang Zhou, also known as Zhuangzi, or Master Zhuang. Writing about 2,300 years ago, he described a dream in which he was a butterfly, fluttering here and there "fulfilling its desires and purposes," and knowing nothing of Zhuang Zhou. Waking up suddenly, he saw plainly that he was Zhuang Zhou, but realized he could not know for certain whether he was truly Zhou, who had just dreamt he was a butterfly, or if he was, in fact, a butterfly now dreaming he was Zhou.

The history master certainly did not have the dreaming sage in mind when he wrote me off as an eleven-year-old lightweight. He was merely saying I had the attention span of an insect, a judgement others have unkindly made since, without considering the virtues of being what British actors call a "quick study." A butterfly mind turned out to be an essential asset for a foreign correspondent who is expected to be on the air speaking in an apparently knowledgeable and sensible way hours after descending into a chaotic and violent situation in a country he's never visited before. The trick is to flit through the enormous amount of information available, events witnessed, and people interviewed, selecting a tiny number of salient points. Each point is like one of the disparate sharply etched dots in an impressionist painting, which make little sense when examined up close but taken together give the illusion of a coherent whole. It is often an obscure yet telling detail, one that would pass unnoticed by a more methodical mind, that makes the result compelling.

As for *Zhuangzi*, the simple parable of the philosopher and the butterfly contains a valuable lesson in the difference between what we know and what we think we know. The first seven chapters of the work, those believed to have been written by Zhuang Zhou himself, have yet to be surpassed in more than two millennia of efforts to observe and describe what it is to be human. The *Zhuangzi* is an exquisitely concise masterpiece of closely observed reporting from the country of the mind.

A typical television report by a foreign correspondent is a miniature painting about two and a half minutes long, often much less. It is a sequence of a couple of dozen shots edited with a voiceover soundtrack containing a total of about 250 words, including those spoken by the interviewees in the two or three soundbites. I make no claim that my efforts to assemble a coherent account of the rough-and-tumble of a day's events have any enduring literary or philosophical value comparable with *Zhuangzi*. Nonetheless, the Chinese classic has given me something to aspire to whenever I sit down and turn loose the butterfly mind to write, whether I am producing one of those 250-word reports or an entire book based on years of them.

I have worked as a foreign correspondent for close to three decades. About half of my career has been spent flitting from country to country, from crisis to crisis. The other half has been spent in China, a country that is the most complex reporting challenge of all. Each of the chapters in this book is divided in that way, too. I have reported on events in almost every country in Europe, the Middle East, and Asia. The first half of each chapter begins in one of those countries. The second half is about China.

I take a particular interest in countries undergoing revolutionary change, either through uprising from within or through outside intervention. I hope that the technique of lining up stories about China beside accounts of events in those other countries might throw some light on the ways in which China is the great exception, and the ways in which it is, in fact, much like everywhere else. I don't offer a closely argued thesis, a carefully constructed argument. The butterfly mind does not work that way. Rather, I invite readers to flit with me through parts of my life, saying to them, "Take a look at that" and "Think about this." I hope this approach, like the dots of a pointillist painting seen from a distance, may produce a different way of understanding, of *seeing* how and why China is the way it is.

There is a third thread woven into the parallel narratives of the book: the story of the chaos of my life as a chronic alcoholic, and my recovery from that chaos. One effect of the attacks on the World Trade Center in 2001 has been to make North Americans interested in conflicts in parts of the world they previously had not paid much attention to. This awareness has led to an increase in the number of journalists assigned to war zones, which has in turn attracted a number of scholars interested in the phenomenon of post-traumatic stress disorder among journalists, and grant money for those who study the condition.

I once attended a presentation by one of these academics, a presentation I found hilarious. He had studied staff at CNN headquarters in Atlanta, Georgia, who had repeatedly viewed images of the 9/11 attacks on television screens in the newsroom. Many of them, he found, were suffering from post-traumatic stress disorder as a result. He had also interviewed a few dozen journalists who had actually been present at a conflict. His study concluded that men who have been to war drink twice as much as those who have not, while women who have reported from war zones drink four times as much as their female colleagues who have stayed home. The implication — that journalists turn into alcoholics and drug addicts as a result of the horrors they witness, either first-hand or while watching television in their newsrooms — has now become part of the folklore passed on in journalism schools. One such school is headed by a former colleague who knows something of my history. Recently, her students have been tracking me down.

"Mr. Brown?"

"Yes."

"I got your name from Professor So-and-so, who says you might be able to help with a term paper I'm working on. It's about trauma and stress."

"Did she tell you I used to drink a lot?"

"Well . . . not exactly . . . but . . ."

I try not to treat these students to a sampling of my irritability and short temper, which in themselves might be interpreted as symptoms of post-traumatic stress disorder. Instead, I explain patiently that I do not believe that alcoholism is an occupational disease brought on by the practice of journalism.

I did not become a drunk because I was a journalist. I became a journalist because I was a drinker. I dabbled in a number of potential careers before finding my vocation in Montreal during the 1970s. Journalism, I discovered, was a job that allowed me to drink during the day. Of course, in 1970s Montreal there was a great deal more tolerance for institutions, such as the long liquid lunch, which are frowned on today, but no other career — except perhaps bartending — came with a licence to drink on the job. My main motivation for becoming a reporter was, I admit, not quite the holy mission to practise a noble craft professed by many people in this line of work. When I stopped being a drunk at the age of forty, I wasn't at all sure that I would be able to practise my profession sober, or enjoy practising it sober. In the event, I carried on being a journalist because I knew how to do it, because it seemed too late to start a new career, and because it turned out that doing it sober was easier and more fun than doing it drunk.

By documenting my years as an active alcoholic struggling to work as an active international journalist I am not trying to make a contribution to the extensive literature of addiction and recovery. The celebrity road to rehab has been well-covered in fact and fiction. I am not a movie actor caught out in a burst of anti-Semitic rage, or a superstar musician drunk and stoned in the spotlight, seeking redemption with a self-promoting litany of confession and remorse. As someone whose work has been public, I suppose I ought to let viewers and listeners know that, more than twenty years ago, I shortchanged them for a long period. But otherwise I see no particular reason why anyone should know or care, unless they themselves have the same problem.

I do want to help people understand that although alcoholism is a fatal, progressive condition that makes us do baffling, stupid, dangerous, and shameful things, there is a solution, and many people have discovered that solution in clinics like the one I eventually found myself in. Alcohol was a friend, comfort, social lubricant, and inspiration for many years. Gradually, drinking became a daily necessity, and ceased to provide the benefits it once had. A source of joy became a source of blackouts, rages, incompetence, incontinence, loneliness, isolation, irrational behaviour, guilt, and remorse. And yet, leaving it behind was as heartbreaking as the loss of a dear friend.

I was trapped in a very dark and puzzling maze. If I had not had help, I do not believe I could have found my own way out. One reason to write about this is to urge anyone similarly trapped to reach out for help. More people would do so, I believe, if there were more public candour about the problem. This is my contribution. I also hope to explain how this experience has coloured my understanding of political change, a key theme of this book.

I spent the 1980s drinking my way through Eastern Europe, the Middle East, and beyond. I was rescued from drowning just in time to witness the events of 1989 in Beijing, Berlin, Prague,

Warsaw, and Bucharest. The turmoil in the communist world followed so quickly on the heels of my own collapse that what had happened to me seemed to be a metaphor for what was happening to societies coming to grips with their own internal conflicts. The foundation for recovery from national darkness and deceit, it seemed to me, was the same as the foundation for personal recovery: honesty, openness, and a willingness to change.

Almost twenty years have passed since then, and in those years China has undergone a dramatic transformation in its economic life. Many other things have improved as a result of the economic transformation, but unlike the Eastern European Communist parties, the party in China has managed to resist political change. If what follows helps anyone to better understand the how and the why of that, and what it might mean for the future, then my desire and purpose will have been fulfilled.

· I ·

CROSSING THE LINE

"If the leadership doesn't like the people, it should elect a
new people."

— BERTOLT BRECHT

Poland's Baltic coast in December 1980 was cold, wet, and grey.
The sky was grey, the rows of identical concrete buildings were
grey, the massive stone churches were grey, and the people's faces
were grey. There was never enough to eat, and scarcely enough
electricity to run streetlights, let alone the neon lights in the empty
shops. The bars were closed. Only the bright red banners of the
free trade union movement Solidarity offered a colourful splash of
hope amid the unremitting gloom of life behind the Iron Curtain.

More than a quarter of a century later, the phrase "behind the
Iron Curtain" has a period feel, evoking an era long ago when we
watched news bulletins on tiny black-and-white televisions and
politicians wore hats, but Sir Winston Churchill's phrase was
inspired shorthand for the vast security apparatus required to
protect the squalid idiocy of a communist state from the light of
common sense.

Solidarity's challenge to communism in Poland was my first
important assignment as a foreign correspondent.

After years of working in Montreal, I had moved to London, the principal base for a breed of reporters known as "firemen." Firemen are constantly on the move, covering news stories that break out in places where there is no resident correspondent. I was thirty-three years old. This move was a promotion to the major leagues of journalism, an opportunity to witness extraordinary happenings. It was also an opportunity to continue my personal self-destruction, a process that was already well underway.

With hindsight, any chain of events takes on an aura of inevitability, but when I scour my jumbled collection of yellowing newspaper clippings and the scripts I filed at the time, I find no hint of the realization that in 1980 we were witnessing the beginning of the end of communism in Europe. Instead, the papers and my own reports were full of speculation that the Soviet Union might invade Poland at any moment to put a stop to change, just as it had invaded Hungary in 1956 and Czechoslovakia in 1968.

Similarly, I had no inkling of the advance of my chronic alcoholism, something I understand today with such clarity. "We can only understand life backwards," wrote the philosopher Søren Kierkegaard, "but we have to live it forwards." Some alcoholics talk about having crossed an invisible line between heavy drinking and alcoholism; others talk about alcoholic drinking from the very first sip. I can see now that for me the die was cast when I was in my teens. I was never going to resist a magic potion that cured shyness and indecision, and created so much spontaneous fun and hilarity. I was sure it was a good and necessary tool for life. At the same time, the key factors in alcoholism are not how much you drink or how much you like it. The heart of the matter is the loss of control, and somewhere between the age of fifteen when I started drinking, and forty when I stopped, I came to the invisible line. Before I crossed that line, I could generally avoid drinking at inappropriate times and in inappropriate ways. After I crossed it, I was no longer in control. The decisive moment, the unconscious commitment to drinking as my top priority, may have happened years before, but it was in Poland that the consequences began to show in my work.

I arrived in Poland shortly after Solidarity was founded in the Lenin shipyard in Gdansk. Reports on the roots of the strike had emphasized the scarcity of food, so I carried in a huge bag of groceries for myself and our interpreters and "fixers," the local people who are indispensable to foreign reporters. The thing I was unprepared for was the drink shortage. The authorities in Gdansk, judging that large crowds are easier to handle when there is no alcohol available, had instituted a temporary Prohibition. I had bought my usual bottle of whisky at the duty-free store at Heathrow Airport, but once that was gone, I had to go without. This was a hardship that I moaned about a lot, but I felt it was an inconvenience rather than a catastrophe, a distinction that would later help me to understand the progressive nature of my alcoholism.

Back in the 1980s, to travel in Eastern Europe was to see what a collection of schoolyard bullies could do to a continent if given control for a few decades. The bullies — the various communist governments — had little reason to suppose their rule would ever end. So the eventual collapse of communism in Eastern Europe came as a surprise, and when it came, it was much more than a transition from economic idiocy to relative common sense, more than a victory for the idea that prosperity is superior to poverty and squalor, more, even, than a transition from dictatorship to democracy, a transition that remains a work-in-progress. It was the triumph of truth over falsehood, and also a triumph of lightness and wit over the doltish and dull.

The Solidarnosc (Solidarity) logo designed by Jerzy Janiszewski, a twenty-nine-year-old artist, was an early sign of the triumph to come. The logo was a vibrant stroke of typographical genius. The urgently scrawled scarlet letters beneath a fluttering Polish flag seemed to be jostling one another in a rush to the barricades, a wonderful contrast to the utilitarian block letters of the Milicja (military police) on the other side. The logo became an instant icon, as recognizable as a Coca-Cola sign or a smiley button, and it was much in demand as a fashion accessory and statement of support around the world.

When I told people before leaving London that I was heading for Poland, almost everyone asked me to bring them back a Solidarity pin. And in Poland, almost everyone wore one. Weeks after the shipyard strike had begun in August, thirteen million people, a third of Poland's total population, were already members of Eastern Europe's first free trade union.

If Solidarity was an instant brand, it also had an instant leader. At a time when Poles were spending half their time forming queues, and all their time hungry, the last straw for the shipyard workers was not what you might expect, the shortage of food. This being Poland, the immediate grievance concerned a commemoration. On August 14, 1980, shipyard workers downed tools to hold a meeting. They were deciding what to do about the dismissal of a colleague, Anna Walentynowicz, who was in trouble with management for complaining about pay and conditions, and for demanding the erection of a monument to workers shot and killed during an earlier confrontation in 1970. Lech Walesa, a thirty-seven-year-old electrician, was getting by doing odd jobs after being fired from the shipyard. When he heard what was going on inside, he jumped over the fence into the yard, joined the meeting, and took control. Solidarity was born.

By December, when I arrived, the authorities had given in to many of Solidarity's demands, including the one that had provoked Anna Walentynowicz's dismissal back in August. An impressive steel monument — three crosses holding up a giant anchor — had been quickly erected outside the number-two gate of the Lenin shipyard, where workers had been shot down during protests over food shortages in 1970.

I attended the dedication ceremony for the monument shortly after my arrival. It was early in the morning, still dark and freezing cold, when crowds began to gather. Special buses and trains brought delegations from factories all over Poland. Groups of coal miners marched through the streets wearing the uniforms and plumed helmets they had first put on for the festival of their patron saint, Saint Barbara, a few days before. Masses had already been held in churches throughout Poland to remember those who were killed in 1970.

The Roman Catholic Church claimed 80 percent of Poles were practising Catholics. Nowhere else in the communist world had organized religion survived as it did in Poland. Even Soviet commissars judged that the Church was too strong to be suppressed. At the same time, the Church was extremely cautious about overt involvement in politics. It claimed to be the guardian of Polish nationhood, culture, history, and language, and often preserved itself by avoiding challenges to Communist Party rule and ignoring communist misrule. In 1980, as the Solidarity movement was gaining momentum, the Church urged moderation and restraint, calling for an end to strikes, which it considered provocative. Homilies preached in those delicate weeks often mentioned the 150th anniversary of an uprising that began on November 29, 1830. Polish military cadets, and then the entire army, had rebelled against rule by the Czar of Russia. The rebellion was ruthlessly crushed and Polish civilians suffered bloody retribution at the hands of Russian troops.

In the endless cycle of invasion, repression, and revolt that makes up the history of this country uncomfortably sandwiched between Germany and Russia, there is always an anniversary to hand when there's a point to be made. No Pole needed to be told that by bringing up the events of 1830, the Church was warning of what Russian tanks in neighbouring Germany and Czechoslovakia would do, if Moscow felt the Solidarity movement was out of control.

At the monument dedication, I stood in intermittent rain with several hundred thousand Poles, including the president, the archbishop of Cracow, and the admiral of the fleet, listening in freezing boredom to hours of speeches. But the cold and rain seemed to disappear when Lech Walesa, a short, wiry man with riveting eyes and a large walrus moustache hanging over a determined jaw, stepped forward. He was one of the most compelling public speakers I have ever heard, even though I couldn't understand a word he said without the aid of an interpreter.

Over the next nine years, I met Walesa several times for interviews and at press conferences, and saw him take part in countless public events. He was one of those extremely rare, charismatic figures who instinctively assumed unquestioned leadership at a particular time and place. In many ways, history has not been kind to Walesa, but in the Poland of the 1980s, he was utterly magnetic. It's hard to imagine how things could have worked out as they did in the absence of such a powerful leader.

Walesa's down-to-earth sense of humour gave him an instant connection with ordinary people, who appreciated his gift for showing up Poland's communist leaders for the selfish, blundering nincompoops they were. He somehow corralled and marshalled a collection of dreamers and rebels, and directed an uprising in slow motion. He united a peaceful army of workers and peasants, and repeatedly pulled back from the brink in the nick of time, while always making sure the brink had moved a little closer to where he eventually wanted to be.

In 1983, he sent his wife to Oslo to pick up the Nobel Peace

Prize, because he was afraid he would never be allowed back home if he went himself. I accompanied him to the airport to greet her when she brought the medal back. I asked him what his next move would be, supposing that he would announce a retreat at the shrine of the Black Madonna in Czestochowa, or some other pious act of thanksgiving. "It's been a while," he said, flinging an arm around his wife, Danuta. "The first thing I have to do is discuss the sacrament of Holy Matrimony with my wife."

Years later, in 1991, after staying with the Queen at Windsor Castle during a state visit to Britain as president of Poland, he emerged with a smirk to say, "The bed was so huge I could hardly find my wife." This upset Polish intellectuals, who felt that he had brought the presidency into disrepute by behaving like a country bumpkin. When it counted, though, he was more like one of those wise and wily peasants in folklore who always outwit the smart city slickers.

The journey from the shipyard gates in Gdansk to Windsor Castle was a difficult and dangerous one, not so much for Walesa, who became such a revered figure that the security services did not dare harm him, but for Poles and Poland in general.

Sixteen months after the birth of Solidarity, I was in Warsaw preparing stories about the prospect of another hungry Christmas and renewed speculation about Soviet intervention. I woke up on the morning of December 13, 1981, to find the telephone in my room in the Hotel Victoria dead and the radio playing martial music. When we went out into the bitter cold of that December morning, my colleagues and I discovered armoured vehicles on the streets. They were not, as we had imagined for so long, Russian tanks. The Polish army had intervened.

Soon General Wojciech Jaruzelski, looking as sinister as any Latin American dictator in dark glasses, was on television explaining the rules of martial law.

We moved around the city trying to find out what was going on. We had no way to file our stories, because the phones were cut off, radio and television transmission stations were shut down, and the airport and the train station closed. It was several days before any of us managed to get reports out of Warsaw. When the international trains finally started running, I joined a small group of British journalists in writing a collective dispatch that a British orchestra conductor, in Poland as part of a cultural-exchange program, agreed to carry on the first train out. It was transcribed into a private code he had devised for taking notes on musical staves. This was journalism of the old school.

With the declaration of martial law, the leaders of Solidarity were arrested along with thousands of activists. The trade union was banned. Several people were killed when security forces opened fire on demonstrators protesting the imposition of what was called in Polish the "state of war."

Martial law was declared on a Sunday, so I went to mass in the Church of the Holy Cross, knowing that this would be where people would gather at a moment of crisis. I stood beside the pillar that contains the embalmed heart of the great Polish composer Frederic Chopin and watched the cold, pinched features of the members of the congregation. Many faces streamed with tears as they sang the country's two great patriotic anthems, "Rota" and "God Save Poland," which have been sung in many different versions over the years, often with words aimed at Germany and Russia, but never before as a prayer for protection from the Polish army.

"Other people have normal countries," said an elderly man standing next to me, his faced deeply etched with lines that seemed to trace the history of the century. "Why not us? Why never us?"

IN THE YEARS that followed the declaration of martial law in Poland, the two sides dug in for a protracted struggle, which I visited often between assignments in Europe, the Middle East, and Asia. Solidarity went underground, and despite the danger, there were frequent protests, often designed as witty and ingenious lampoons of a heavy-handed regime. On one occasion, I saw helium balloons painted with the Solidarity logo released inside the cavernous hall of the Palace of Culture, a huge Stalinist building that looked like a giant, cement wedding cake and boasted an observation deck said to have the best view in Warsaw, because it was the only place in town where you could look over the city without seeing the Palace of Culture. It had been built as an unwelcome "gift" from the Soviet Union. The Solidarity balloons bobbed gaily around the lofty ceiling as officials tried to swat them with sticks. Another day, what seemed to be the entire output of an electronic resistor factory appeared on people's lapels, the brightly coloured cylinders symbolizing "resistance" now that Solidarity pins were banned. Sometimes, walking down the street in the evening would feel like a stroll through a huge electronics showroom, because everyone had put their television set in the window facing outwards. It was a highly visible and witty rejection of the propaganda broadcast read on the nightly news by a detested announcer in military uniform.

During one of the occasional periods of liberalization, the veteran comedian Jan Pietrzak was allowed to reopen his cabaret for evenings of sketches and stand-up about food and freedom of speech. "A woman goes into a butcher's shop and asks, 'Do you have any pork chops today?' 'Niema,' says the butcher. 'How about lamb?' 'Niema!' 'Beef?' 'Chicken?' 'Sausage?' 'Niema!' She leaves and the butcher turns to his assistant. 'Crazy old bitch, but what an incredible memory!' Two dogs meet at the East German border. The Polish dog asks the German dog why he's headed for Warsaw.

'I hear you can bark there. Why are you going to Berlin?' 'Because I hear you can eat there. It's great being able to open your mouth, but it's even better to have something to put in it.'"

Two men from the censor bureau sat at a special table beside the stage, taking notes and bellowing with laughter. The show was closed down a few days later.

In 1979, Karol Josef Wojtyla became Pope John Paul II — the first Polish pope. In June 1983, his visit to Poland gave an enormous boost to the opposition, and an equally enormous headache for the authorities.

State visits of any kind can be extremely gruelling for journalists, but the visit of this energetic pope to his homeland was exceptionally tough. Every morning the Pope's activities began early, and so did the various statements back and forth about what he was saying and doing, all of which had to be reported. Getting from one city to the next was a logistical challenge, and travelling gobbled up hours of most days. The Pope celebrated mass late into every evening. Colossal crowds made traffic impossible for everyone except the Pope in his helicopter, so the trudge from the evening mass back to a press centre where we journalists could file our reports would often take until the early hours of the morning. Filing itself would take a couple of hours, and then it would be time to leave for the next city. And so it went, around the clock for eight days in a row.

Having been caught unprepared by the imposition of Prohibition during my first visit to Poland in 1980, I knew that the authorities would ban the sale of alcohol for the entirety of the Pope's visit. As a precaution, I packed six bottles of Glenfiddich single-malt Scotch in my suitcase.

Like many alcoholics, I was truly unaware of the creeping progression of my drinking, and it did not occur to me that six bottles for eight days was a lot. It seemed about the right amount. When I noticed that I was drinking heavily, I told myself it was only a temporary response to a specific situation, and things would soon be back to normal. In reality, by 1983, being drunk every single day had become normal for me. It was while I was covering the Pope's visit to Poland that I started to drink as soon as I woke up. My rationalization for this was that I was getting so little sleep that I needed something to kick-start the morning. Then, of course, it was necessary to have a sip or two from time to time throughout the day to keep going. In the event, six bottles was not enough, and I foraged for more, finding corrupt hotel employees and black marketeers here and there to supplement my supply.

My notebooks from trips to Poland between 1980 and 1989 reveal the steady advance of my alcoholism. In 1980, I thought of myself as a serious drinker, but not a problem one. My employers were sufficiently unaware of its effects on my performance to appoint me to a much sought-after job. I had a reputation for hard drinking, but I thought of this as part of the image I worked hard to project: I liked to think of myself as an old-school journalist heading toward the sound of gunfire armed with a battered portable typewriter and a bottle of Scotch. The 1980 notebooks have copious notes in relatively clear handwriting. They are a reasonable record of a diligent journalist's work, although they do give an indication of many a drunken night. One entry, in extremely large, wobbly letters, with many exclamation points for emphasis, records a decision to give up thinking about learning the language. "Polish impossible!! Gin and Tonic masculine! Whisky feminine! Beer neuter! *Jedn Gintonic. Jedna Visky. Jedno Piwo!* No wonder Poles good at other languages and nobody else learns theirs."

By the time of the Pope's visit in 1983, the notes had become increasingly sketchy, and my notebooks from later years are almost impossible to decipher. After I stopped drinking, my handwriting never reverted to clear legibility. Heavy drinking does permanent damage.

Considering that I was drinking around the clock and grabbing catnaps on buses and planes, my scripts from the Pope's visit were really quite good. The crowds that turned out to see him in each of the eight cities he visited numbered in the millions. He gave homilies, sermons, or speeches on twenty separate occasions, and wrote all of them himself. He refused the Polish government's request to vet them.

When he arrived at the airport in Warsaw, the Pope began by quoting Matthew 25:36: "I was in prison, and ye came to me." That evening in Saint John's Cathedral, he went on to describe his fellow countrymen as "feeling the bitter taste of disillusion, humiliation, and deprivation of freedom." Almost every time he spoke, he would be interrupted by tumultuous applause, especially as he contrived to use the word "solidarity" repeatedly in one context or another, such as, to give just one example, "the solidarity of the brotherhood of man."

After granting separate audiences to Lech Walesa and General Jaruzelski, the Pope called on the government to resume negotiations with the workers and restore the reforms suspended by martial law. The Polish government, in return, accused the Pope of breaking an agreement that the visit should be exclusively religious and moral in content. In the diplomatic tradition of ignoring the truth to keep up appearances, the head of the Vatican press office, Father Romeo Panciroli, responded with a statement that read: "One notes attempts by some international mass media to interpret the Pope's trip and words on the basis of their content suggesting intentions of a political character. Nothing could run more counter to the intentions of His Holiness. . . ." I wrote a report on the statement suggesting that Father Panciroli's confessor might impose a penance for the sin of bearing false witness.

After decades of judging that compromise, even complicity, with the communist regime served Church interests better than support for opposition to communist rule, the Church had finally taken sides. And the Church led by a Polish pope was a vital source of moral and practical support. Solidarity was banned, but churches provided ready-made meeting places in every neighbourhood and rallying points for the commemoration of countless anniversaries that provided a focus for perpetual protest. The Church also had the capacity to maintain a national organization under its wing. It was the biggest and most efficient institution in the country.

As the stalemate continued, I was sent to Poland less often, but when I did go, I always spent a lot of time in church. After the Pope's visit, one particular priest attracted attention. Father Jerzy Popieluszko's sermons were uncompromising attacks on the government. Attending a service at his parish church, Saint Stanislaus Kostka in Warsaw, was rather like being at a revival meeting, with guitars, drums, and lots of applause. Father Popieluszko was a handsome, dynamic man who could have been a rock star or a tel-evangelist in another time or place. In Poland, he became a martyr.

In October 1984, he was on his way home from a visit to the town of Bydgoszcz in northern Poland when he was stopped at a roadblock and bundled into the trunk of a police car. His battered body was found floating in a reservoir ten days later. It was the sort of "disappearance" that is an unremarkable feature of dictatorships of the right and the left around the world. This being Poland, and Father Popieluszko being a priest, it provoked universal outrage, and a national crisis which the government was able to defuse only by the arrest and trial of the four policemen said to be responsible. The incident illustrated perfectly the capacity of the opposition to confront the brutality of the regime and the inability of either to prevail.

The event that would eventually lead to a break in the stalemate took place in Moscow on March 10, 1985, when the Soviet leader Konstantin Chernenko died of heart failure brought on by emphysema and cirrhosis of the liver. He was the last of the dinosaurs. The front page of the Soviet newspaper *Pravda* the next day announced that Chernenko would be replaced by fifty-four-year-old Mikhail Gorbachev. All the conditions were now in place for Poland to be the first East European country to make a break with communism.

Poland had a coherent and united opposition movement with a charismatic leader and a clear message summed up in its one-word name. Unique among communist countries, Poland had the support of a powerful non-communist institution in the shape of the Catholic Church, as well as an influential voice in world affairs in the person of the Pope. The relentless food shortages and the dismal greyness of life in Poland guaranteed the existence of a vast majority eager to join in any effort to put an end to communist rule. And finally, in the Soviet Union, which had built the entire ramshackle edifice of East European communism, power was now in the hands of a man who would decide not to use military force to preserve it.

By 1989, even the government seemed to have lost the will to keep the whole sad charade going. General Jaruzelski had followed Gorbachev's example by introducing limited Polish versions of the Soviet liberalizations known as "glasnost" and "perestroika," but whatever good this had done for the government's position was undone by an exponential increase in public dissatisfaction, and demands for more concessions. Solidarity began a final push, and in February agreed to "round-table" talks on the future of the country, which led to the government's fatal promise of limited elections in June.

At the same time, after ten bloody years of trying to extend its empire into central Asia, the Soviet Union was about to withdraw its troops from Afghanistan. Gorbachev would give any East European leader who asked him the question a fraternal socialist kiss on both cheeks and whisper that he was not going to send the troops in anywhere else. Jaruzelski was on his own.

My first task on my last visit to Poland in 1989 was to report on yet another commemoration in Gdansk. Dignitaries and surviving participants gathered to remember the opening shots fired on the city by the German battleship *Schleswig-Holstein,* in the early hours of the morning of September 1, 1939: the beginning of the Second World War. The miserable chain of events set off by the shots fired fifty years earlier was about to reach a turning point. Twelve days after the ceremony in Gdansk, I was in the parliament, the Sejm, watching Tadeusz Mazoviecky being sworn in as the first non-communist prime minister of Poland since the war.

Solidarity had fought the election in June with its characteristic flair and élan. Instead of using a picture of Lech Walesa, or reaching back into Polish history, or basing its campaign on a pedestrian catalogue of the failings of communist rule, Solidarity called up the image of one of the greatest of Hollywood westerns, which had always been popular in Poland. The election poster showed a publicity still of Gary Cooper wearing a Solidarity badge above his sheriff's star, accompanied by the slogan, "June 4 It's High Noon." The voters got the message, and on election day, June 4, 1989, they banded together (unlike the townsfolk in the film *High Noon*) and began the job of dismantling communism.

In that election, Solidarity won all but one of the one hundred seats in the senate, and all of the seats in the lower house that it had been allowed to contest, one-third of the total. By setting limits on the number of seats the opposition could contest, the Communist Party had hoped to guarantee itself a permanent majority, but it was tripped up by the decision taken years before to set up sham political parties, so as to be able to claim the rubber-stamp parliament was democratic. In a rare moment of genuine poetic justice, the peasants and the democrats had switched to the Solidarity camp, and the "Party" was over.

I was supposed to cover that election, but missed it. For as long as calendars are marked with anniversaries, the Polish election will be a footnote, and June 4, 1989 will be remembered, not for what happened in Poland that day, but for what happened in China.

———•———

IN MAY 1989, as I was pushing my way through a horde of students on Tiananmen Square, a young man stopped me and said, "Would you like to meet China's Lech Walesa?"

He led me to a tent pitched on the northwest corner of the square and introduced me to Han Dongfang, the spokesperson for the Beijing Autonomous Workers Union. Han Dongfang is a tall man with a wonderfully persuasive, rich, deep voice, and an unshakeable conviction that his cause is just, and will one day prevail. As soon as I heard his voice, it struck me that he would make a marvellous radio talk-show host.

I was also struck by the odd coincidence that Han Dongfang was an electrician, like Lech Walesa. He had worked for the railway, travelling around the country maintaining refrigerated wagons. A former soldier, he had served for three years in the prison service of the People's Armed Police, a branch of the army. When he was detained later, one of his prison guards recognized him from having served in the same unit.

Han Dongfang was not a natural rebel or dissident. Even his name is testimony to his parents' communist conformity. Dongfang, meaning "the east," is taken from the Maoist anthem, "The East is Red." He had volunteered for the army, and later applied several times for membership in the Communist Party, but was turned down. He says he was finally disillusioned with the system, after he witnessed protestors being beaten up by police, during earlier student demonstrations in Beijing in 1987. Today, he gives the impression that if only the party had lived up to its promise of brotherhood, equality, and a better life for workers and peasants, he would still be working on the railway.

Even before I met Han Dongfang in Tiananmen Square, the situation in China struck me as familiar. Here was a communist country in the grip of enormous, passionate demonstrations demanding change. Here was martial law. And here was a free trade union set up to challenge the Communist Party's claim to represent the workers. But the similarities between what was happening in China and what had happened in Poland were quite misleading, and it turned out that the membership of the Beijing Autonomous Workers Union never rose above double figures.

In Poland, Solidarity was an instant challenge to communist rule. What began as a notion cooked up by a few disgruntled shipyard workers became within days a national institution. Solidarity quickly had millions more members than the party itself. By the end of August 1980, the authorities had capitulated to many Solidarity demands, including concessions that anticipated the eventual end of communist rule. The concessions were reversed for a while by martial law, and it took the remainder of the decade for the party finally to admit defeat, but the writing was on the wall for those able to read it — in big red letters with a Polish flag fluttering defiantly above them.

In China it was students, not workers, who first raised their voices. The demonstrations began on April 16, in response to the death of the former Communist Party leader Hu Yaobang, who had collapsed from a heart attack during a politburo meeting the day before. He had kept his politburo seat when he lost his position as general secretary of the Communist Party over his handling of the previous student demonstrations in 1987. He was generally supposed to have been in favour of reform, so his death was an ideal opportunity to raise the issue again.

In China, paying respect to a dead leader often provided the pretext for criticizing, either obliquely or directly, the conduct of living ones, but this time conditions were ripe for a prolonged crisis. Paralysis at the top prevented the quick, decisive response that would have nipped the protests in the bud. At the same time, people really were angry about the corruption and hypocrisy of the party.

Another important factor was the impending visit of the Soviet leader, Mikhail Gorbachev. On the one hand, his efforts to reform the Soviet Union provided a focus for anyone in China who was thinking that change was needed. And on the other hand, Gorbachev would be accompanied by a large number of journalists and their cameras, so that anything that happened would be guaranteed world media attention. Gorbachev's visit to the Great Hall of the People would signal the end to more than a quarter of a century of hostility between Beijing and Moscow. The rapprochement was interesting to be sure, but the spontaneous combustion taking place on the streets outside was much more compelling.

No one working for a news organization could ignore the Gorbachev visit completely, but like the rest of the pack, I was concentrating my attention on the protests. My script from the day Gorbachev and the Chinese supreme leader Deng Xiaoping sat down for a banquet reveals how badly I misread the event. I made much of the image of the younger Gorbachev grappling vigorously, if clumsily, with his chopsticks, while Deng Xiaoping feebly used his to transport the odd morsel with trembling hands to his tortoise-like face. I used the two images as an extended metaphor for their relative strength, and probable future, writing about Gorbachev as a confident reformer at the height of his powers, and Deng as a feeble old man in the twilight of his.

The reality was quite different. Gorbachev and the Soviet Union would be gone in a couple of years, while Deng was about to assert his grip on China through the ruthless use of military force, then follow that up by launching a second economic revolution at the beginning of 1992. He would remain the unchallenged supreme leader of the country until his death in 1997.

Outside the Great Hall, the clamour for less corruption and more openness had struck a chord that resonated with vast numbers of Chinese. They quietly shared a widely held view, one that young people had the audacity to voice out loud: that officials who preached socialist austerity for everyone else had grown shockingly rich themselves. The mood was one of support for the young idealists who dared say in public what many had been saying in private during a decade of economic reform. People thought the party should come clean in more ways than one. "Sell your Mercedes and Pay the National Debt!" was a popular slogan.

One of the most important things people were asking for was greater transparency. When, on April 26, the *People's Daily* published an editorial denouncing the protests as counter-revolutionary, the next day the protestors were back in even larger numbers and with renewed vigour, screaming one of the dullest slogans I've ever heard: "Retract the *People's Daily* Editorial of April 26!" During many attempts to talk the students back into their campuses, officials acknowledged that they had made good points, and that the party and government should address them. Deng Xiaoping himself said that not a hair of the students' heads would be harmed.

Student activism was not new to China, and a convenient anniversary presented itself on May 4, a red-letter day in the calendars of both the Communist Party and of reform-minded Chinese. The date was a landmark in China's struggle to reverse the nineteenth-century depredations of the Western powers. On May 4,

1919, students had staged large demonstrations in front of the Tiananmen Gate to protest against the results of the Versailles Conference. The students were outraged by the humiliating news that the great powers had decided to award the German "concession" in Shandong to Japan instead of returning it to Chinese sovereignty.

Now, seventy years later, students marched to the Tiananmen Gate knowing this anniversary would afford them a degree of tolerance and licence. It was obvious to all Chinese, but not to me at the time, that the same tolerance would not be accorded to rebellious peasants or workers. When Han Dongfang, and his handful of fellow workers who thought the time was ripe for the establishment of a free trade union, approached student leaders, the students refused to permit them to join the main protest in Tiananmen Square. Instead, they allowed the trade unionists to set up a small ghetto on the northwest corner of the square, on the fringes of the main demonstration.

In Poland, the formation of a free trade union had led to the imposition of martial law. In China, it was the imposition of martial law that sparked the creation of a free trade union. Han Dongfang says that he and "about fifty or a hundred" others formed the Beijing Autonomous Workers Union a few hours after Premier Li Peng declared martial law on May 19. They held elections for a five-person committee, and chose Han Dongfang as spokesperson. It was one of those moments that changes a person's life forever, like Lech Walesa's decision to clamber over the shipyard fence.

Meanwhile the students' inspired tactic of a hunger strike, combined with public resentment over the clumsy declaration of martial law, provoked even bigger demonstrations. People from all walks of life were now turning out to support the students. Tiananmen Square is supposed to hold at least a million people. It has been estimated that three million people took part in the demonstrations at their height. During one of the big turnouts after martial law was declared, I walked about seven kilometres along the wide boulevard from the square to the television station, pushing through crowds of people jammed shoulder-to-shoulder all the way. The overpass that crosses Beijing's second ring road was clogged with trucks and buses bringing people into the centre of the city. They brandished banners and flags, blew horns, and banged drums and cymbals. The cavalcade included large numbers of ordinary workers waving banners that echoed the students' slogans, and others announcing the name of the factory or work unit they came from. It was as if truckloads of delegates were going to some gigantic convention, or workers in hundreds of factories and offices were all heading for a picnic in the same place at the same time. People were enjoying every minute of the escape from routine drudgery, laughing, cracking jokes, and making a deafening racket as they went. Ordinary citizens far outnumbered the students. It felt like an enormous street party. There was, without a doubt, a great deal of admiration and support for the students, and sympathy for their demands, but Chinese friends who were there suggest that *qihong*, the Beijing impulse to join a boisterous crowd to see what's going on, was a major motivation too.

Hardly anyone who went down to the square was interested in joining the Beijing Autonomous Workers Union. People passed by the tent in their millions, but only a few dozen signed up. "When we approached people asking if they wanted to join our organization, they would step back, saying they were just there to support the students, they didn't want complications," said Han Dongfang. "This was partly a hangover from the Cultural Revolution, when being part of a counter-revolutionary organization was far worse than being declared a counter-revolutionary individual, so people would take part as individuals, and not take responsibility."

One of the few things I got exactly right during this first visit to China was an on-camera stand-up I did in the square on May 24. Some art students constructed a giant plaster replica of the Statue of Liberty, which they renamed the "Goddess of Democracy" and hauled onto the square. The statue became the focus of the protests. Loudspeakers were blaring "Ode to Joy" from the last movement of Beethoven's *Ninth Symphony* just as a violent thunderstorm struck. The music, the wind, and the rain combined to drive the huge crowd into a frenzy. The storm cast an eerie light over the apocalyptic scene. Struggling to make myself heard above the noise, I told viewers that the statue of an American icon in front of the Great Hall of the People was a provocation the authorities could not possibly tolerate, while warning of bloodshed if they tried to remove it by force.

I still feel pangs of regret when I recall what happened next. As if my memory of what I had seen and said for the past month had been completely erased, I made no protest of my own when, a few days later, my editors decided the story was winding down. The anniversary of May 4, the indignation about the *People's Daily* editorial, the emotional appeal of a hunger strike in a country where food is an obsession and many citizens had personal experience of famine, and the excitement over the Goddess of Democracy had all come and gone. There was no new inspiration. Many students, too, felt the protests had run their course, and that it was time to withdraw, leaving the authorities with the embarrassing task of dismantling the statue. Only a few hundred remained in the square each night. There were too many reporters in Beijing with too little to report, and things were happening elsewhere in the world. Those of us who had flown in were ordered back to our bases, and I left for London.

When I got home, I had not even taken off my coat before one of my sons dragged me to the television set to see images of

Chinese soldiers squatting with their hands behind their heads in Tiananmen Square, captured, disarmed, and humiliated by students. I turned around and headed back to Heathrow, knowing that a terrible vengeance was inevitable.

I arrived back in Beijing on the morning of June 5, and made my way downtown through back streets still echoing with gunfire. There I began reporting on the aftermath of the massacre, wondering how I could have been so stupid as to leave when I did.

It was painful to be in Beijing in the weeks that followed. There was a large appetite for news from China, and no way to report it properly. People who used to grab us eagerly in the street to explain what they thought would now walk stonily past without making eye contact. It was impossible to talk to anyone, and impossible to film anything worthwhile. Beijing was swarming with soldiers. There were police, both in uniform and in plain clothes, everywhere. Satellite transmissions had been cut, so our usual method of editing reports on location and transmitting them before airtime was no longer possible. Instead, we developed a system for producing our on-camera stand-ups a day early. Each morning we would use guesswork and vagueness to film a stand-up that we hoped would be relevant to whatever might happen in the day to come. A courier would carry the cassette on a flight to Hong Kong. I would sleep for a few hours during the day, then get up in time for the 7:00 p.m. newscast on China Central Television (CCTV), which was also recorded in Hong Kong and transmitted to our headquarters along with the pre-recorded stand-up.

The CCTV news was a depressing daily diary of the crackdown, with the faces of the most wanted, news of arrests, and pictures of dead and injured soldiers and burned-out vehicles. It also included political statements and announcements. I would stay up through the night, filing reports for radio and daytime television on the other side of the world. And later, I would try to tie together whatever snippets of information we had managed to gather, the CCTV pictures and the stand-up we had sent almost twenty-four hours earlier, into a coherent narrative for our own nightly newscast. Once the script was agreed with editors back home, I would read it over the phone, have breakfast, and go out to film another stand-up, beginning the whole dismal and frustrating process over again.

Much of the reporting from China in 1989 portrayed the Beijing students as so many Paul Reveres on bicycles, young revolutionaries poised to bring change to China right then and there. I like to think that I saw things a little more clearly than that, but probably I didn't. It seems to me now, when I look at China in relation to other places, that I was often unable to distinguish where China was different from the rest of the world, and where it was the same. China is regarded, and regards itself, as the great exception, and so it is. Sometimes. At other times, once surface appearances are discounted, things happen for much the same reasons as elsewhere, and people behave much the same as they do anywhere else. The problem is that it is hard to judge at any given moment whether one is witnessing the unique or the universal.

By the end of 1989, blinded perhaps by so often writing the words "protest" and "Communist Party" in the same sentence, I assumed that China had been part of a worldwide movement to shrug off communist rule. I thought that the process had only been delayed by the willingness of the authorities to shoot down students on the main square of the capital, but that it would inevitably resume and end in the same way as elsewhere. I was fascinated by the prospect of the movement beginning again, and when the opportunity came, I moved to China, imagining that I would soon see Chinese communism's demise. Almost twenty years later, I am still waiting.

At the height of the demonstrations, three men, Lu Decheng,

Yu Zhijian, and Yu Dongyue, threw paint bombs at the giant portrait of Mao Zedong that hangs over the Tiananmen Gate. Horrified by the sacrilege, and fearful that it might compromise their movement, the students grabbed the three and handed them over to the police. The three paint-bombers were jailed for counter-revolutionary sabotage.

The incident illustrates a key point. Throughout Eastern Europe, communist rule was regarded as a result of outside intervention by the Soviet Union. China's Communist Party had Soviet advisers, and followed the model of organization developed in the Soviet Union, but it came to power in a home-grown revolution. Marxist theory was changed and adapted to suit Chinese conditions, abandoning, among other things, the Soviet emphasis on the urban proletariat because of the vastly greater significance of the peasant population in China. By June 1989, the boilerplate introduction to any Chinese political speech would always include the phrase, "Marxist-Leninist Mao Zedong thought and Deng Xiaoping's important theory of Socialism with Chinese Characteristics," as a kind of "Made in China" pedigree for whatever party line followed. In 1989, the behaviour of the party was in question, its legitimacy was not. The Tiananmen Square protestors, including Han Dongfang, were seeking reform, not revolution.

When the army assault on the square had begun on the night of June 3, Han Dongfang was still manning the union tent. He remembers a group of young people coming to the tent at about 11:30 p.m. They compared him with Lech Walesa and urged him to leave with them. He insisted on staying until they came back a second time and picked him up bodily, carried him out of the tent, then surrounded him as they walked past a burning tank, heading eastward away from the gunfire and out of the square.

IN THE EARLY HOURS of the morning of June 4, Han Dongfang left Beijing alone, on a bicycle, with a vague plan to cycle around the country meeting groups of workers and peasants to spread the word of what had happened in Tiananmen Square, but a nation-wide crackdown had already begun. He soon saw his face on the television news alongside the pictures of the most-wanted student organizers, and decided to return to Beijing to face the music. Back in April, when he had been elected to the five-member committee of the Beijing Autonomous Workers Union, he had checked with a law student to make sure that the creation of a free trade union was legal and constitutional. One quality Han Dongfang shares with many Chinese dissidents and activists I have met is a naive and dogmatic insistence on the letter of the law, coupled with an absolute conviction that he is in the right, that the system and the people who apply it are in the wrong, and that the logic of the situation requires that he will be vindicated. He turned himself over to the authorities, when others on the most-wanted list were scrambling to escape from China, because he believed it was the right thing to do.

The Chinese legal tradition places great emphasis on confession and contrition. A favourite party maxim, *tan bai cong kuan, kang ju cong yan*, sums it up: "Leniency for those who confess, severity for those who refuse." Han Dongfang was subjected to days and nights of sleep deprivation and psychological torture in the battle of wills between him and his interrogators over whether or not his decision to walk into the police station should be described as "giving himself up." He insisted that he had walked into the Public Security headquarters to take responsibility for his actions, not to surrender. He saw maintaining the distinction as a matter of principle, crucial to the integrity of his conduct throughout.

After twenty-two months in prison, Han Dongfang was released for medical treatment in the United States, in one of those deals China makes with Western politicians, letting a prominent prisoner go as a concession on the eve of some state visit, or ceremony, or international decision involving China. The practice is the moral equivalent of hostage-taking, the difference being merely a matter of the timing of the detention, pay-off, and release. Han Dongfang is the sort of person who might have refused to take part, had he not been so ill with tuberculosis and other conditions brought on by mistreatment in jail. Even so, he did promise his family he would come back soon, and he did his best to keep that promise.

As soon as he was released from hospital in the United States, having lost his damaged lung but regained his health under treatment, he flew to Hong Kong and began using it as a base for repeated attempts to go back. He was turned away every time he presented himself at the border, and eventually he realized that he could not go home. He settled in Hong Kong.

"I realized it wasn't my job simply to make the Chinese government look bad by trying to cross the border every two weeks surrounded by reporters," he explains. "I had to go back to my original purpose, which was to help create a workers' movement."

Han Dongfang was not allowed to return to China, but in 1997 China came to him. A few months before China regained sovereignty over Hong Kong, after a century of British rule, I went to see him to talk about the handover. He was one of the people I referred to as the "canaries in the coal mine" — individuals whose treatment under Chinese rule would be the test of Beijing's willingness to keep its promise of "one country two systems." This was the guarantee China had made, that Hong Kong people would continue to run Hong Kong, with its laws, institutions, and freedoms intact, for at least fifty years.

With help from Hong Kong trade unionists and human rights activists, Han Dongfang had started a newsletter, *China Labour*

Bulletin, in 1994. In March 1997, a few months before the Hong Kong handover, he began broadcasting a radio program into China twice a week on Radio Free Asia, a program that now claims an audience in the millions.

Listeners phone in about all manner of labour problems, talking about poor pay, dangerous conditions, and strikes that habitually end with police intervention and the arrest of anyone suspected of being a ringleader or organizer. By phoning officials in China, and telling them that he is calling from the *China Labour Bulletin*, he elicits some amazingly informative interviews with people who assume they are talking to a reporter from an officially sanctioned publication.

China has trade unions, of course, like any communist country. Their job is not to represent the workers, but rather to help the management keep the workers in line. That applies just as much to the private corporations, and to foreign companies doing business in China, as it does to the state-run enterprises. Indeed, the case of Wal-Mart is extremely revealing. The retailer not only buys much of what it sells to the rest of the world in China, it also is opening megastores in China itself. A company which in other jurisdictions has preferred to shut down, rather than allow union membership, agreed when the government suggested it should allow union branches in its facilities in China. Although it is ferociously opposed to unions everywhere else in the world, Wal-Mart simply sees an official Chinese trade union as no threat whatever.

LECH WALESA'S MOMENT of decision in 1980 was followed by years of struggle, and then by an extraordinary victory for the movement he led. His path has taken him to the presidential palace in Warsaw and back to Gdansk for a comfortable, smug retirement.

In 2005, in an interview marking the twenty-fifth anniversary of the birth of Solidarity, Walesa, by then the former president of Poland, said, "Poland broke the bear's teeth so that it could not bite others. Pope John Paul II should take 50 percent of the credit for that, Lech Walesa and Solidarity 30 percent. The rest can be divided among others."

By 2005, the righteous intensity of the young activist who had climbed the shipyard fence to lead a revolution was scarcely discernible. Walesa was an autocratic disappointment as president, and Solidarity itself lost its heart when it became part of the establishment, instead of a quixotic opposition movement.

Walesa was right in saying that it took an historic alignment of a number of factors and personalities to "break the bear's teeth," and the end of communism in Eastern Europe could not have happened if any element had been missing. The Pope, Walesa, and Solidarity were prime movers, and the courage of those who were willing to risk their lives and liberty is undeniable. Nevertheless, the key was the bear's decision not to bite. Things would have been very different had the Soviet Union been willing to intervene, or had the Polish army been willing to use consistent and ruthless lethal force.

In contrast, Han Dongfang's single-minded struggle for workers' rights continues to this day without any measurable success. The Chinese Communist Party will not tolerate any breach in its monopoly on power, and the creation of independent trade unions is a development party leaders will resist until they have no choice but to make concessions. They know that if they share power they will quickly lose it.

Other protestors who came to prominence in Tiananmen Square in those tumultuous weeks of 1989 are now scattered around the world. Some have moved on, while others keep themselves busy with the impotent irrelevance of exile politics, arguing with history and one another. Han Dongfang sits behind the microphone in a sterile, beige radio studio in Hong Kong, reaching out with his velvet voice to people in the sweatshops and mines of a homeland he can't get back to, keeping faith with the speech he made in May 1989, asking a few dozen people to elect him to the committee of the new Beijing Autonomous Workers Union.

In summer 2006, Han Dongfang and I were panellists at an earnest conference on "Rights and Democracy in Asia" in Toronto. There was much introspection and debate about what foreign governments, non-governmental organizations, and individuals must do to promote democracy in Asia, and to bring about the creation of free trade unions in China. Han Dongfang picked up the microphone with a sigh. "You really can't do anything," he said. "And why, by the way, do you suppose it is your responsibility to change China? In the end it is up to Chinese workers themselves to demand their rights, and eventually they will succeed."

· 2 ·

CHAOS

> "Civilization begins with order, grows with liberty, and dies with chaos."

— WILL DURANT

One of the most ominous sounds you will ever hear is the crash of shop shutters coming down in Beirut. The first rattle and bang of one shop closing is joined by the horns and racing engines of cars trying to flee, and this is the cue for a whole percussion section to join in as all the shopkeepers in the neighbourhood shut down. There is a final clang as the last shutter is rammed home. People develop a remarkable instinct for impending trouble in a city at war. In one of my occasional recurring dreams of Lebanon, I hear that sound in the distance as I walk down a deserted street strewn with rubble. The menacing silence after the last shutter falls is followed by a gunshot, or the roar of a car bomb, or the whistle and crump of a shell landing nearby, then smoke darkens the bright Mediterranean sunshine, and there is blood, and screaming. But much more often in my fleeting dreams of war, I find myself in the place I spent much of my time in Beirut — in the bar of the Commodore Hotel.

This dingy, no-star hotel had been the headquarters of the

world's press, since it was discovered by journalists retreating from fighting around their previous five-star havens in the old city, at the beginning of the civil war. The attraction of the Commodore was the relative safety of the neighbourhood, and the hotel's magical ability to keep electricity, telephone, and telex connections when all around were losing theirs. As the war dragged on, the management and staff became adept at negotiating with all factions, and arranging all manner of media logistics, including help from time to time with the release of detained or kidnapped journalists. The Commodore was a useful institution for all sides, each of whom could find us easily when they wanted to communicate their point of view to the rest of the world. The hotel led a charmed life for many years before finally being overrun and destroyed during fighting between rival Muslim factions in 1987.

It is commonly supposed that some journalists drink heavily because of the dangerous and irregular lives they lead, but I am absolutely sure that, in my case at least, this is back-to-front. If I had been a bank manager or a bishop I would still have been a drunk. I was not drinking because of what war was doing to me. On the contrary, one of the reasons I liked going to wars was that it gave me a licence and an excuse to drink. I relished the unpredictable turmoil of a country at war, and the sense that doing a job in a war zone not only entitled me to respect, it also relieved me of any responsibility for anything outside the zone. Simply to be in Lebanon was to exist in a privileged bubble, absolved from the mundane chores of normal life. And the bar of the Commodore was a bubble within the bubble, a place of total ease and comfort, where the camaraderie of war conferred the right to drink as, and when, one pleased, chattering and laughing about close calls on the front line, with a full glass in hand, and another one on the way. I went to Lebanon several times a year between 1981 and 1985, tracking the chaotic progress of a failed state, and descending deeper into personal chaos. By 1983, the wake-up drink I had become used to, when following the Pope in Poland during the summer, had become a regular part of my morning routine. I was now more or less drunk all the time, and was to stay that way for another four years.

I first learned the meaning of the shop shutters crashing down in 1981, in a Christian neighbourhood called Ain al-Rummaneh. The latest round in Lebanon's recurring civil war was already six years old by that time, and I was in the neighbourhood to take a look at the place where it had all begun. I had arrived in the country a couple of days previously to cover a crisis over the installation of some Syrian long-range missiles in Lebanon. Israel was taking exception to the move, insisting that the Syrians remove the missiles or else the Israeli air force would do it for them. The Lebanese, I learned, often suffer two kinds of war at once: one they inflict on themselves and another that outsiders inflict on them. After I had driven out to the Bekaa Valley to take a look at the silver-and-white rockets pointing south, I did not have much else to do until something dramatic happened, or the crisis worked itself out in the diplomatic back-and-forth between Jerusalem, Damascus, Washington, and elsewhere. I tried to keep myself busy, and so the visit to Ain al-Rummaneh became part of an introductory crash course in what happens when a country falls apart.

The war had started with a drive-by shooting on April 13, 1975. Unidentified gunmen had fired at a church from a speeding car. In retaliation, Christian militiamen ambushed a busload of Palestinians, killing twenty-seven. It was not much of a massacre by the grisly standards set later, but added to the clashes and assassinations that had gone before, it was enough to tip the country over the edge.

On the day I visited in 1981, my plan to talk to people about the place where the war had begun was interrupted by the noise of the shutters and my driver's insistence that we leave immediately. A few minutes later, shells began falling. We crossed over the Green Line that separated Muslim West Beirut from the Christian East just before it closed for several days of routine mutual bombardment.

On that same trip in 1981, I also went to look at the bridge of the Nahr al-Kalb, the Dog River, just north of Beirut. Long ago, it formed the border between the Egyptian and Hittite empires. When he passed through with his army three thousand years ago, Egypt's Ramses II had put up a monument there, beginning a tradition followed by subsequent military expeditions to Lebanon. The Assyrians, the Romans, the Crusaders, the French under Napoleon III, and in modern times, the French again, and the British are among those who left a record of their passing.

Ain al-Rummaneh and Nahr al-Kalb together sum up Lebanon's double curse: civil war and foreign interference. Many neighbours and foreign powers have had a hand in Lebanon over the centuries, but the last outsiders to make a serious stab at actually running the country were the French. France took control of Lebanon in 1918, after the Ottoman Empire was dismantled by the First World War, and stayed until 1943. The French had had a relationship with Lebanon's Christians since the Crusades, and an enduring legacy of French rule was a political structure frozen by an unwritten agreement known as the "national covenant," which made sure Christians ended up with the lion's share of political and economic power. The national covenant includes a power-sharing formula based on a census carried out under the French in 1932, the last census anyone had the courage and the will to conduct.

In accordance with the terms of the covenant, official positions are shared out among eighteen recognized sects, in proportion to their numbers in the census. Of course, the numbers are wildly out of line with the makeup of the population today. Even in 1932, the census results were probably tweaked in favour of the Maronite

Christians, a Roman Catholic sect that is specific to Lebanon, and named after Saint Maron, a fourth-century monk. The power-sharing formula was set without any workable way of adjusting it. Even today, the presidency must always go to a Maronite, the prime minister's office belongs to the Sunni Muslim community, the speaker must be a Shiite, while other offices must go to the Druze and Orthodox sects, and so on, through all the ministries, governorates, municipalities, and the civil service. It may have been a workable compromise at the time, but subsequent changes in the relative strength of Christian, Sunni, and Shia populations have made it the cause of enormous death and destruction.

The problem was compounded by the arrival of large numbers of Palestinian refugees, mostly Muslims, after the founding of the state of Israel in 1947. Refugee camps became armed states within the state, and the Palestinians brought with them their guerrilla war against Israel. They won sympathy from Lebanese Muslims, but Christians resented them, not least because their actions against Israel brought reprisals that affected Lebanon as a whole.

The civil war started as a fight between Christian militias on the one hand, and Palestinians allied with Muslims on the other. With the changing music of events, the war became a macabre quadrille, with alliances and partners changing frequently. New dancers arrived from outside from time to time, adding to the complexity of the figures, so that at one time or another all the Christian sects have fought one another in addition to fighting Muslims. Muslims have slaughtered each other as well as fighting Christians, and rival Palestinian groups have had their own civil wars on Lebanese territory. Each faction has been armed and encouraged by rival regional powers or international sponsors.

This penumbra between civilizations and religions, a place where Europe and the Middle East, Christianity and Islam overlap, has influences from so many historical currents, and so many ethnic and linguistic groups, that wider quarrels can be fought out on a small scale. Any nation or cause, near or far, can find a proxy in Lebanon.

That first visit was one of the very few times that I managed to fly into Beirut's battered airport. Usually, by the time I needed to get there, the airport had been closed by whatever crisis I had been assigned to cover, and I had to travel overland from Syria or by boat from Cyprus. My first time, however, I arrived directly from Rome, where I had been covering the assassination attempt against the Pope not long after he returned from Poland. The Pope had been shot three times on May 13 by a deranged Turkish gunman in the most serious of several attempts on his life. Now that the Pope was recovering, however, he was old news, superseded by the Syrian missile crisis and fears of a Middle Eastern war. Ordered to try to get on the afternoon flight to Beirut, I rushed to the Lebanese embassy in Rome to secure a visa, in the process giving myself the smart line for later use: that the most dangerous thing I did that year was to tell a Rome taxi driver to hurry up.

Within a couple of days of arriving in Beirut, I was cheerfully pontificating from the confident posture of one pretending he has seen it all: "The situation in Lebanon would be bewildering even for a student of the Byzantine Empire or eleventh-century Italy," I wrote, as if I had reported from both. "The continuing hostility among Israel and the Arab states is compounded by a series of changing alliances and conflicts between more than forty armies and militias on the ground: the Tigers of Chamoun, the Falangist Kataeb, the Marxist Palestinians, the Moribaitoun, Palestinians who follow the thought of the late Gamal Abdel Nasser, as well as the PLO, the Syrian army, and the Lebanese army."

Although my tone implied deep understanding of complex issues, I have never been an expert on anything. I have spent my life going from place to place, always in a hurry, watching other people do things, and writing and talking about what they are doing. Before I moved to China, I was never anywhere long enough to feel that I fully understood what was happening. Even now, I am always on the outside looking in.

Back in the early 1980s, I revelled in constant movement. I was almost never home, and when I was I wanted to be somewhere else. It was on my second trip to Lebanon, during the Israeli invasion of 1982 and the ensuing siege of West Beirut, that I really found the voice of the person I wanted to pretend to be. That voice had the weary swagger of someone pushing beyond normal limits, living life on the edge, saddened by the violence around him, but somehow rising above it all to send dispatches from the belly of the beast. I arrived in Beirut in the spring of 1982 after being grounded in London for months, reporting on another war, the one between Britain and Argentina, that was happening thousands of miles away in the South Atlantic. No glory in that.

Only British reporters had been allowed to join the Falklands campaign. The rest of us were chained to our desks for twenty hours a day waiting for lugubrious and gnomic Ministry of Defence briefings that were the only way to track the progress of the war. When I was heading homeward in a cab one night, I was held up by the blue flashing lights of a police cordon around the Dorchester Hotel on Park Lane. The police told me it was a serious shooting incident. I made some phone calls when I got home and filed a story reporting that Israel's ambassador to Britain had been shot by a Palestinian armed with an automatic rifle. The last line read, "A man is critically ill in a London hospital. More lives may be at risk in southern Lebanon, the obvious target for an Israeli counterstrike." Israeli preparations for war in Lebanon had been common knowledge for months. With the shooting in London, the *casus belli* had arrived. I knew it was time to be on the road again.

My Beirut-bound flight the next day was diverted to Cyprus. After waiting through the night, hoping Beirut airport would reopen, colleagues travelling with me opted to head for Israel, to cover the impending war from there. I decided to take my chances with a group of Lebanese people I had met at the hotel bar who were planning to find a boat. We took a freighter bound for Beirut the next night. Most of the passengers stayed on deck, but I found an open chain locker in the bow with a tarpaulin to curl up in. There I listened to my radio and sipped from a bottle of Scotch before getting a good night's sleep. I was awoken by anxious shouts just after dawn. Our ship was within sight of the coast of Lebanon and an Israeli gunboat was approaching fast. The captain pulled out an Israeli flag and began waving it from the bridge, shouting that we were Lebanese civilians going home. We were allowed to pass, and I was in the Commodore Hotel before nightfall.

As soon as the Israeli ambassador had been shot in London, it was obvious there was going to be trouble in Lebanon, but I had no idea it would be a full-scale invasion. Israeli forces made an alliance with the Lebanese Christians and stormed up through southern Lebanon to East Beirut. The Muslim west side of the city was soon under siege.

My days were organized around Canadian radio deadlines. I would usually get up early, and go out to gather material for reports that I would file before noon, in plenty of time for early morning radio newscasts in Canada. In the age before the Internet changed everything, all information had to be collected in person, or else culled from the Reuters teletype machine that chattered away in the lobby of the hotel, or gathered from the radio. Wherever journalists congregated, every hour on the hour, a little forest of antennas would flip up in time for the strains of "Lilibulero," the theme tune of the BBC World Service news. The Lebanese had their ears glued to local stations.

Those sources would provide the context and often the main news of the day: how many killed and wounded, how much territory gained and lost, what diplomatic efforts were being made to bring an end to the fighting, what repercussions the war was having elsewhere. Whatever I found when I went out, interviews with local leaders and ordinary people, visits to hospitals or vignettes of the fighting, would serve to add life, colour, and observed detail to my dispatches. Sometimes these bits of local reporting were strong enough to stand on their own.

In 1982, there were no laptops, no cellphones, and no satellite phones. The only way to file my reports was to get back to the Commodore early enough to call them in through the hotel switchboard. By ten in the morning, I would be in my room knocking out my first script on a portable typewriter, then I would head downstairs to connect my tape recorder to the hotel phone line to file the story quickly. I would make the morning news and be in the bar by noon.

I was not alone. Drinkers find each other, and alcoholic drinkers are a generous source of support, rationalization, and justification for one another. The crowd around the bar was a mix of aid workers, war tourists, young freelancers trying to make a mark, chancers, spies, arms dealers, conmen, and diplomats. Among the journalists, some were Arabists who had devoted their lives to understanding the region. Others lived from war to war. Many had come here in 1975, after the fall of Saigon, because it was the best war going, and later would move on to the Balkans after interludes in El Salvador and Nicaragua. As a "fireman," I would spend several weeks at a time in Lebanon, until things became relatively calm, and I was assigned to some other crisis in some other country, only to rush back when something big happened. In 1982, members of the Palestine Liberation Organization (PLO) and their leader, Yasser Arafat, agreed to leave West Beirut; the Israelis lifted their siege of the city but continued their occupation; the Christian president-elect, Bachir Gemayel, was assassinated by a huge bomb;

and Israelis allowed Christian militiamen to enter the Sabra and Chatilla refugee camps where they massacred the Palestinians there who had been left unprotected by the departure of the PLO.

Then things got really complicated. A multinational peace-keeping force of American, French, British, and Italian troops was deployed, the Israelis moved out, and the Syrians moved in. While these six sets of outsiders, and other countries like Iran, which maintained proxy militias, were showing what the presence of foreign forces could do to Lebanon, the Lebanese also continued to show what they could do to themselves.

The Israelis retreated all the way back to their buffer zone in southern Lebanon in September 1983. There was an immediate settling of accounts among the Lebanese who lived in the Chouf mountains above Beirut. A year of Israeli occupation had upset the local balance of power, and the two sects that have lived in, and fought over, those mountains for centuries began slaughtering each other again.

The best-selling book at the Commodore Hotel bookshop was a reprint of a book that had been first published in 1862, *The Druzes and the Maronites Under the Turkish Rule from 1840 to 1860.* Its author was Colonel Charles Henry Spencer Churchill, a British army officer who was in Lebanon during an earlier war between the Maronite Christians and the Druze, a secretive Muslim sect that broke away from the Muslim mainstream in the eleventh century. Like many minorities elsewhere in the world, the Druze had managed to survive by retreating to inaccessible mountain terrain. Among the many peculiarities of the Druze faith are a belief in reincarnation and the conviction that there are millions of adherents living secretly in China, who will form a huge Druze army when Christian and Muslim forces meet in a final Armageddon in Mecca. The Druze believe that both Christianity and Islam will be defeated with the help of their Chinese brothers.

Churchill's account of the 1860 massacres was uncanny because the names of key players and the places they were fighting over hadn't changed, and the savagery of the fighting hadn't changed either. In 1983, the villages and towns of the Chouf looked about the same as they had in 1860. "The slaughter next commenced," Churchill wrote, and continued:

> Whenever a Christian was seen, he was shot or cut down. Flames at the same time burst forth in various places. Dark smoke was brooding over the town. The shouting, swearing and screaming was appalling. . . . It's now become clear that this first attempt of the Maronite Patriarch and his colleagues to establish an exclusive ascendancy in the Lebanon by weakening if not destroying the Druze element has signally failed. The emptiness of their boastful taunts and denunciations were fully exposed. Their lofty and ill-judged schemes of aggrandizement had completely miscarried.

Druze and Maronites were unfamiliar to most of the world, and the resumption of their centuries-old vendetta would have won little attention were it not for the presence of the Israelis, the Syrians, and the multinational peacekeeping force in the middle of their vicious little turf war, which made the whole bloody mess seem somehow more significant. Then in October 1983, a Shia suicide bomber drove a truckload of explosives into the American base near the airport, killing 241 Marines. Another bomb killed fifty-eight French soldiers at their base. The peacekeeping force, which had seemed like such a good idea, began to pull out. Two weeks later, on October 31, the leaders of nine principal Lebanese factions met in Geneva to talk peace. They had to meet in Switzerland because there was no way to guarantee their security in Lebanon.

Their arrival in overcoats and dark glasses brought to mind any number of movies about the Mafia.

During this time, the war in Lebanon generated a great deal of interest in war journalism, and what it was like to work in such extreme conditions. This provided me with an opportunity for self-indulgent reporting that I find quite shameful today. At the time, though, I imagined that I was part of a new wave that combined the sensibilities of rock 'n' roll with the Grand Guignol realities of war-without-rules in the video age. Near what used to be the heart of downtown Beirut, where weeds grew among buildings so riddled with holes they looked as though they were made of lace, I spotted a billboard advertising "Eddie Cooper's Full-Tilt Roller Boogie Disco Show." This became a favourite metaphor in my reporting, especially after the billboard was blown to smithereens by a shell.

When I review my work in Lebanon over the five years from 1981 to 1985, I can see a clear progression, much like what I found in my notebooks from Poland. My earliest reports reveal a conscientious effort to come to grips with a complex and difficult story, and to report it in a compelling way that was sympathetic to the people caught up in the violence without being either sentimental or mawkish. By 1982, my style had begun to change, taking on a tone of self-satisfied bravado. As my drinking progressed, my reporting became more and more an exercise in self-promotion. The situations I was talking about became a backdrop, and the people became extras in a narrative designed, not to make the audience understand what was happening, but to admire the reporter who dared to be there. The most important words were the sign-off, "Patrick Brown, Beirut."

Here's part of what I wrote about the peace talks in Geneva:

We journalists can say who they were, and what they were doing — this group of warlords, thugs, gangsters, old chieftains, and young heirs to the sins and burdens of their assassinated fathers and brothers, the eternal optimists who have watched the country fall apart, and the eternal meddlers become "observers" who have helped it all to happen — but it takes a poet to get to the murky depths of it all. W. B. Yeats, who died in 1939, never set foot in Lebanon, but he wrote often about Ireland, a country that comes close to Lebanon in the major leagues of places where sectarian hatred, long memories, and stubborn insistence on revenge have congealed together to make a sticky mess all the dishwashers in Christendom, or Islam, couldn't scrape from the bottom of a dirty pan. Watching the old men in Geneva, who even with the leavening effect of newcomers like [Bachir's brother] Amine Gemayel and [Druze leader] Walid Jumblatt had a combined age of 572, I could not help but recall Yeats's line: "Bald heads, forgetful of their sins."

On and on it went, winding up with:

Each of the nine Lebanese leaders in Geneva this week came with a peace plan. Syria has a hard line and peace plan, Ronald Reagan has a peace plan, Israel has a firm threat and a peace plan, even the Soviet Union thinks it has something to gain. Everyone has a plan, but only the poet has the answer: "Too long a sacrifice can make a stone of the heart."

Much of the time I was not reporting any more. Armed with borrowed lines from the *Oxford Dictionary of Quotations*, I was posturing and pontificating, writing from the point of view of an imagined character who was war-weary and sensitive, yet tough.

Memories of my last trip to Beirut in 1985 are a kaleidoscopic blur. Shia militants hijacked TWA Flight 847 en route from Athens to Rome, and diverted the plane to Beirut. As the days went by, the plane flew back and forth to Algiers a couple of times, while the hijackers murdered one passenger and released several others in groups, until there were thirty-nine left, all American citizens. The Shia militia Amal, which by that time had won control of most of West Beirut, stepped in, representing itself as a mediator. Amal fighters took the hostages off the plane and transported them to secret locations in the city, to prevent any rescue attempts.

Since 1982, a couple of dozen Westerners had been kidnapped in Beirut, mostly diplomats, journalists, and teachers, but also the CIA station chief William Buckley, who was eventually murdered, and Terry Waite, the special envoy of the Archbishop of Canterbury, who was eventually released. The addition of thirty-nine American travellers to the missing list attracted a media circus. Many news organizations had stopped sending reporters to Lebanon because of the kidnappings, but now I was joined at the bar of the Commodore by a swarm of new drinkers.

Four o'clock in the morning would find me hanging on to the piano screeching improvised greatest hits for hostages: "Please Release Me!," "Some Islamic Evening," "Shia'll be Coming Round the Mountain," and so on. When the Amal leader, Nabih Berri, in his imperfect English, said the hostages were passing the time "playing sports," we roared all night over the idea of the hostage Olympics, with events such as the grenade-and-spoon race. I was still finding time to file reports, but most of my days and nights were spent in this fantasy world in which we answered the threat of death with the camaraderie and hilarity of those who dared to be there, and had the licence to kick all the chocks out from normal behaviour, because of where we were and what we were doing, sending inspired dispatches from a world gone mad.

I cherished anecdotes that I supposed illustrated our insouciant intrepidity. One night, when gunmen started shooting in the hotel lobby, one of the bartenders leaned toward the pillar I was hiding behind and said, "Don't worry, Mr. Patrick, it's only gangsters." Another day, I arrived at the Defence Ministry offices during an incoming mortar attack to be greeted by a guard who said, "Sir, here you are not safe." Yet another time, seven people were killed in street fighting between militias controlled respectively by the minister of justice, Nabih Berri, and the minister of public works and tourism, Walid Jumblatt. One night we held a Yasser Arafat look-alike contest. Another night, two French photographers broke their legs while celebrating selling a picture for the cover of an international newsmagazine. The first leapt into the empty swimming pool and then his friend jumped in to save him.

I was proud of what I was doing. When a magazine asked me for a piece about reporting from Lebanon, I wrote:

> Amal's military commander for West Beirut, Aql Hammieh, wandered into the Commodore Hotel surrounded by gun-toting bodyguards just after the American hostages had been released. Having a can of beer in my left hand, and a large cognac and a cigarette in my right, I was a little non-plussed when he came over to shake my hand. With what little aplomb I could muster, I piled cognac upon beer, squeezed the cigarette in between, and said, "I'm sorry Aql, I'm not feeling very Islamic tonight." It was another triumph of diplomacy. He laughed.

Others worked in these conditions with courage, dignity, and good judgement, doing a dangerous but honest day's work. I was utterly wrapped up in self-centred drama, sitting in my room after the bar had closed, drinking and listening to a Tom Waits song, "Tom Traubert's Blues," over and over again on my cassette recorder. "And it's a battered old suitcase to a hotel someplace . . . where everything's broken and no one speaks English . . . ."

Finally, on June 30, 1985, the hostages were released with a grotesque farewell party hosted by one of the American television networks at a seafront hotel. The next morning I came downstairs to find the place deserted. I had given no thought to the probability that with the crisis resolved, the informal moratorium on kidnapping had expired. I was lucky enough to find an American network team heading for a charter plane, and they were happy to have an extra Canadian passport to wave out of the window as we went through the dozens of checkpoints that had already sprung up along the airport road.

When I was asked why I continued to cover the world's conflicts, my standard response was that I was not attracted to the violence or excitement of war, but to the unique opportunity to witness the extremes of human behaviour, good and bad. I would usually cite a story I did in 1983 about a school for blind children in Beirut. When the battleship USS *New Jersey* was firing shells famously described as being "the size of Volkswagens" over the city, the children were taken down into the basement with the school orchestra's instruments, so that they could play music to drown out the noise of the explosions, which were especially frightening for blind children because of their heightened sensitivity to sound.

Simplistic posturing covers up a multitude of sins. The truth was, I enjoyed war because it gave me the opportunity to play the role of a person who would give an answer like that and mean it.

———

A GREAT OBSESSION of China's leaders is the fear that China will become like Lebanon. They certainly don't express it that way, and would be insulted or amused to hear anyone compare China, which they perceive to be a vast, united nation enjoying unprecedented peace and prosperity, to Lebanon, which they see as an insignificant little country, the size of a Chinese city district, with a quarrelsome population. Still, the overriding preoccupation of Chinese Communist Party leaders, who want above all to remain in power, is the fear of internal disintegration and interference from outside. Those are the things that have turned their country into a giant version of Lebanon many times in the past, within living memory as well as in ancient times.

One afternoon in 1995, I watched Li Xiuying chop French beans for dinner. Her broad features were deeply lined and oddly uneven, her eyes half-closed under heavy lids.

"Now I am old, the wrinkles have covered up my scars," she said, as she sliced each bean into pieces and flipped the pieces aggressively into a bowl. She spoke in the same steady rhythm as the strokes of her knife. "I can't forget it. For my entire life until I die I won't forget it," she said.

On her business card, on the spot where most people have a company name and title, Li Xiuying had "Survivor of Nanjing Massacre during Japanese Invasion of China."

Japan's occupation of China had begun in 1931, when it set up the puppet state of Manchukuo in Manchuria in northeast China. The expansion into the rest of China started in 1937.

Li Xiuying was nineteen years old and seven months pregnant in December 1937 when Japanese troops marched into Nanjing. Because she feared that an arduous journey in wartime might cause her to lose the baby, she said goodbye to her husband as he sat on the roof of a troop train leaving the city, along with the Chinese Nationalist government, which abandoned its capital in the face of the Japanese advance.

After her husband left, Li Xiuying and her father moved into an elementary school that had been turned into a refugee camp in the part of the city called the Nanjing Safety Zone. It was organized by a committee of the twenty-two missionaries and businessmen who had stayed behind when most of the foreign community fled. People inside the Safety Zone fared much better than those outside, but during their six-week orgy of killing and rape, the Japanese committed atrocities throughout the city, including inside the Safety Zone. The exact figures are a matter of dispute, but historians estimate that at least 150,000 civilians were killed, and tens of thousands of women were raped. China's official estimate is more than 300,000 dead.

Li Xiuying was caught by a group of Japanese soldiers who entered the school on December 18. When she fought back, she was stabbed thirty-seven times, raped, and left for dead. She was taken to Nanjing University hospital, where surgeons patched her up. John Magee, an American Episcopal missionary, took pictures of her appalling injuries with his home-movie camera. Magee's film of Li Xiuying and other victims adds moving visual evidence to the compelling written accounts of Chinese survivors and foreign witnesses. And yet, to this day, there are Japanese who claim the Nanjing Massacre never happened.

Li Xiuying was particularly outraged by the Japanese denial of what happened in Nanjing. When Japanese writer Toshio Matsumura accused her of fabricating her story in his book, *The Big Question in the Nanjing Massacre*, she sued him and won her case in a Tokyo court in 2003.

"Winning my lawsuit dealt a severe blow to the Japanese right wing and represented a victory for all survivors of the massacre. I believe that the truth never ceases being the truth, nor vice versa. Attempts by the rightists to deny historical facts will always fail," she said, even as Matsumura perpetuated that denial by lodging an appeal. Li Xiuyang died in December 2004, six weeks before the Japanese Supreme Court ruled, at last, that the Nanjing Massacre really did happen, and that she was a victim of it.

In 1995, cooking dinner as she talked to me, she had attacked the beans as if they were those soldiers of sixty years before. "I can tell you that in Nanjing every family lost someone, relatives or friends," she said.

"And . . . "

Chop!

"we all . . . "

Chop!

"*hate* . . . "

Chop!

"the Japanese!"

The Chinese authorities overcome their deep dislike of public protest on rare occasions when it suits the government's purpose to highlight a particular issue. Japan's reluctance to confront its wartime conduct is one such issue. Large crowds sometimes materialize outside Japanese diplomatic and commercial premises to protest visits by Japanese politicians to the Yasukuni shrine in Tokyo, where they pay homage to Japan's war dead, including a number of war criminals. Disputes over offshore islands and oil resources, or the wording of Japanese textbooks, can also create tension. If Japanese schools whitewash history, Chinese education makes sure no one forgets it. Bitter memories live on among people born fifty years after the Nanjing Massacre.

"We're particularly disgusted by the way they changed the school textbooks," one teenage schoolgirl told me at a demonstration in Beijing in 2005. "Invading China, then denying it, that's not right!"

"They should apologize," said another.

At the same time, self-interest can trump indignation. In 1972, Mao Zedong waived any further reparations in exchange for Japan's diplomatic recognition, economic aid, and a lukewarm apology that Japan "deeply reproaches itself."

During the furor over textbooks, I met a Nissan dealer at one of Beijing's car markets who was torn between her resentments and her livelihood. Liu Fengqin said she would continue selling Japanese cars, but would stop buying other Japanese products. "I'm joining the boycott," she told me. "I'm switching my brand of face cream to a Chinese one."

Business is business, and Japan and China do lots of it, but on an emotional level there is a hunger for Japanese contrition, a hunger that repeated apologies can never satisfy. In a speech in August 1995, on the fiftieth anniversary of the end of the war, Japan's Prime Minister Tomiichi Murayama was typically vague about the events he was apologizing for: "During a certain period in the not-too-distant past," he began, trying to avoid upsetting the atrocity-deniers by not mentioning the Second World War by name. After more evasion and circumlocution, he did eventually offer this outright apology: "In the hope that no such mistake be made in the future, I regard, in a spirit of humility, these irrefutable facts of history, and express here once again my feelings of deep remorse and state my heartfelt apology."

Around the time of this apology, in February 1994, I went to see Dr. Ken Yuasa at his small clinic in Tokyo, where he was still practising medicine at the age of seventy-eight. Someone had told me his story at a dinner party, and I was keen to interview him for a report on Japanese attitudes to the war.

"If I lived in any other country, I would be barred from medical practice," he said. "But here in Japan, the only thing I am criticized for is speaking out about what I did."

Dr. Yuasa went to China in 1942, as a twenty-six-year-old doctor in the Japanese army, and he began his career as a war criminal by using Chinese prisoners as live subjects for teaching surgical techniques. "We used two at a time, blindfolding them, then shooting them in the stomach, so we could practise surgery," he said.

"Most died on the table. Those who survived the operations, I killed with an injection."

Yuasa also says he conducted experiments at the request of Japanese pharmaceutical companies and cultivated typhoid bacilli that he believes were intended for poisoning wells in areas where there was Chinese resistance to the occupation.

Yuasa was captured and held in China as a war criminal until 1956, but he remains shocked by Western indifference to the use of tens of thousands of Chinese as guinea pigs in medical experiments, including large-scale germ warfare tests. "German doctors who did this sort of thing to other Europeans were hanged," he said. "Because we were Asians doing it to other Asians, the Americans didn't think it was important."

We wanted to include some shots of Dr. Yuasa's daily life outside the clinic, but he said if he were seen being filmed outside, he would have problems with neighbours who resented his frankness about the atrocities he had seen and committed. Apologies for Japan's wartime behaviour in China are controversial in both countries. They are resented by many Japanese, and rejected by many Chinese.

Patriotic fervour was allowed on the streets of Beijing over a different issue in May 1999. American bombs had fallen on the Chinese embassy in Belgrade, killing three journalists and injuring twenty others, during the crisis over the former Yugoslav province of Kosovo. The United States insisted the bombing was a mistake, but many Chinese were convinced it had been deliberate.

I found myself in the middle of the biggest demonstrations Beijing had seen since 1989, and for the first time ever in China, I felt threatened by a hostile crowd. I had to explain loudly and often that I was Canadian, not American, and brandish my passport at angry protestors who took a moment from throwing rocks, eggs, and paint-bombs at the American embassy to turn their attention to me. There were similar demonstrations at consulates through-out China. In Chengdu, the mob set fire to the American consul's residence.

In Beijing, the authorities not only provided buses to transport students from their universities on the other side of town, but they also assigned large numbers of police to maintain crowd control and make sure the long lineups of people waiting their turn to throw things at the embassy kept moving in an orderly fashion.

The United States maintained that the embassy building in Belgrade had been targeted because intelligence based on old maps mistakenly identified it as a military facility. This explanation was ignored completely. For three days, China's President Jiang Zemin refused to accept phone calls from U.S. President Bill Clinton, and Chinese officials in Washington and Beijing rejected frantic over-tures from their American counterparts. The Chinese people were told through newspapers, radio, and television that the bombing of the Belgrade embassy was a brazen and deliberate act of aggression, for which no apology had been given. The word "regret" used in early American statements was dismissed as inadequate to the occasion. "It's the kind of thing you say when you step on some-one's foot," said one Chinese official.

Chinese patriotism is deep, sincere, and extremely powerful. The authorities harness it when they can. When people feel that China has been insulted, or when there is a wave of pride over an achievement like a space shot, or a sporting triumph, party leaders wrap themselves in the flag, and their popularity is stoked by the reflected warmth of popular feeling. They also worry that they will lose stature if their response to any crisis is insufficiently patriotic. President Jiang, a particularly vain and pompous man, who was extremely sensitive over his lack of military credentials compared with his revolutionary predecessors, could not afford to show weakness in the face of foreign bullying. When, on the fourth day of the crisis, it was judged that sufficient indignation had been expressed, and that angry demonstrations might slip out of control, Jiang accepted Clinton's call. Clinton's statement afterward was shown on Chinese television, and the protests came to an end.

"I have already offered my apologies to President Jiang and the Chinese people," Clinton said. Exceptionally, Chinese television showed the clip of Clinton with subtitles, instead of the usual announcer voice-over translation, so that everyone could clearly hear him utter the word "apologies."

In 2001, demonstrators were outside the United States embassy again after an American Lockheed EP-3 reconnaissance plane and a Chinese J-8 fighter jet collided over the South China Sea.

American spy planes conducting surveillance missions and probing Chinese defences dance daily with Chinese fighters trying to chase them away. This frequently leads to near misses, and the risk of collision is increased when hot-dogging pilots try to impress one another. On this occasion, the Americans claimed the Chinese jet came too close and clipped the lumbering EP-3's wing. The Chinese said the EP-3 swerved into the path of the J-8. Whoever was to blame, the Chinese fighter plane was sliced in half, and pilot Wang Wei ejected into the sea. His body was never recovered, despite a vast search that eventually covered more than 750 thousand square kilometres of sea. The EP-3 was damaged, and made an emergency landing at the nearest airport, which happened to be in China's island province, Hainan. The crew of twenty-one American servicemen and three servicewomen was held for eleven days while the dictionaries came out.

China demanded a formal apology. The United States refused to apologize for anything, expressing only "regret" for the loss of the Chinese pilot. The Chinese, with twenty-four hostages and a plane full of spy equipment in their custody, had the upper hand. President George W. Bush answered a letter from Wang Wei's wife who had written accusing him of cowardice for not apologizing. He used the word "sorry" for the first time, but officials insisted he was offering condolences to the pilot's family, not apologizing for the collision, or the plane's spy mission.

"Sorry" brought a concession from Jiang Zemin, who accepted that the collision had been an accident, but he continued to insist on an apology. "I have visited many countries, and I see that when people have an accident, the two groups involved, they always say excuse me," said Jiang. "American planes come to our borders and they don't say excuse me. This sort of conduct is not acceptable in any country," he said.

There were two days of argument over whether the United States should use the word *baoqian* to say they were sorry or the more formal and regretful *daoqian*. In the end, the United States offered, and China accepted, what became known as "the letter of the two sorries." It said that the United States was "very sorry" about the death of Wang Wei, and expressed "sincere regret" about the loss of the aircraft. The crisis was over.

The decision to release the American crew was announced late at night. I wanted to include reaction from ordinary citizens in my report, so I waited until daylight, and then went out to interview people on their way to work. I had come to China to cover the crisis, but I had been living elsewhere for some time. It had been several years since I had done any man-in-the-street interviews, and I was quite surprised by what I heard.

Whenever I had done these "streeters" in the past, people who disagreed with the government were uncertain about the official line, or did not want to stick their necks out by talking to a foreign television team would walk briskly past, refusing to comment. Anyone who did stop to talk for the camera would trot out the official line, often quoting the day's newspaper editorial word-for-word. This time, the first eight people I stopped all were willing to talk. Four agreed with the government's resolution of the crisis, but four disagreed.

"The Americans apologized. We won," said one man.

"The government should not have accepted this," retorted a woman standing behind him. "The Americans should not have been allowed just to say 'sorry' and walk away."

To be sure, the difference of opinion was between very patriotic and even more patriotic, which was entirely in keeping with Chinese attitudes toward any perceived slight or injury to the country's dignity and sovereignty. What struck me was that all the people I spoke to, not only believed they had a right to a personal opinion about the government's conduct, and were willing to express it publicly in a foreign television interview, but they also were willing to voice a critical view.

It was a significant change. Since 1989, there has been a major expansion of freedom of thought and expression on many issues. People talk openly about all sorts of things that used to be taboo. It is only when it comes to anything the Communist Party considers a threat to stability or its own monopoly on power that the security apparatus is as rigid as ever. The fear of losing control, of chaos real or imagined, trumps everything.

THERE IS NO ancient Chinese curse that says, "May you live in interesting times!" The assertion that there is such a curse has become an enduring cliché of political commentary and speechmaking throughout the Western world. The first person I heard say these words was Canadian Prime Minister Pierre Elliott Trudeau during an election campaign in the 1970s. His speechwriters probably grabbed it from a speech American President John F. Kennedy gave in South Africa in 1966, and *his* speechwriters probably pinched it from someone who lifted it from "U-Turn," a 1950 science-fiction story by Duncan H. Munro. What is certain is that no Chinese person, either ancient or modern, ever uttered such a curse.

The myth owes part of its endurance to the stereotype of Chinese inscrutability. In reality, the Chinese swear they are, by and large, just as "scrutable" as the rest of us. "Stupid cunt! Fuck your uncle!" is the sort of thing you hear when a traffic incident escalates into a public show.

There seem to be fewer scatological references in Chinese than in English profanity, though I have fond memories of an old gentleman in a village on the upper reaches of the Yangtze River who, when I asked him a question, shook his stick at me and called me a "farting devil!"

Chinese cursing is largely sexual, with a characteristic emphasis on illegitimacy and ancestry — not surprisingly, given the reverence paid to ancestors in Chinese tradition. "Fuck your ancestors to the eighteenth generation!" is a little recherché for use on the street, but "turtle's egg" and "son of a rabbit" are in common use, implying bastardy because of the supposed promiscuity of the animals invoked. "Your mother's . . ." and "Go to your grandmother's . . ." are handy insults for everyday use.

Although it does not actually exist, the "interesting times" curse does resonate with Chinese attitudes. There is a deeply held view that stable government, no matter how flawed, is better than chaos. And the fear of *luan*, "chaos," is central to Chinese political life. In the long sweep of China's history, periods of political consolidation and prosperity have often been followed by fragmentation. Stable dynastic rule was toppled by rebellion, internal strife, or invasion.

To give just one example, the Tang Dynasty, founded in 618, saw the expansion of Chinese territory into Korea and Vietnam in the east, and central Asia in the west. Commerce, literature, and the fine arts flourished. The capital, Changan, today's Xian, was the greatest cosmopolitan city in the world, more than three times the size of ancient Rome.

Then came the decline, which the historian John King Fairbank describes as "an object lesson in anarchy. Officials, both civil and military, became so cynically corrupt and village peasants so ruthlessly oppressed that the abominable became commonplace. Loyalty disappeared, banditry took over. Gangs swelled into armed mobs plundering all in their path as they roamed from province to province." That lasted for about a hundred years, until China's descent into general warlordism was resolved by the installation of a new dynasty, the Song, that established a new golden age, the equivalent of the Renaissance in Europe.

The rise and fall of great dynasties, punctuated by periods of disintegration and anarchy, has engrained in Chinese thought a sense of history as a cyclical process. Some of these chaotic interludes were a very long time ago, but there are people still living who remember the end of what was perhaps the greatest upheaval of all.

The period from 1841 to 1949 is known in China as "the century of humiliation." Some observers argue that the period of humiliation began earlier and lasted longer, but the turning point is generally agreed to be the cession of Hong Kong to Britain during the Opium War. Fighting began in 1839, and in 1840 Britain invaded China to defend the lucrative opium trade, which the last imperial dynasty, the Qing, was trying to suppress. The British victory led to more land grabs by foreign powers, the Boxer Rebellion, the overthrow of the Qing dynasty, the invasion and occupation by Japan, warlordism, civil war, and finally the victory of the Communist Party in uniting all of mainland China. "The Chinese people have stood up," declared Mao Zedong from the Tiananmen Gate of the former imperial palace, the Forbidden City, on October 1, 1949.

It is customary to see rule by the Chinese Communist Party as monolithic and unchanging, but under Chairman Mao, the relatively short period of stability after the founding of the People's Republic was followed by chaotic political campaigns that lasted, one after the other, for nineteen years. The Great Leap Forward, from 1958 to 1960, probably caused the greatest loss of life, with thirty million deaths by famine, while the Great Proletarian Cultural Revolution from 1966 to 1976 was the longest and most disruptive.

In the past century and a half, there have been fewer than thirty years of relative stability, starting in 1979 with Deng Xiaoping's policy of reform and openness. Even this period was interrupted by the massacre of student protesters in 1989. The *People's Daily* editorial of April 26, 1989, which so inflamed the students who were demanding more openness and less corruption, used the word *luan* over and over, as it outlined the justification for the eventual crackdown: "Their purpose was to sow dissension among the people, plunge the whole country into chaos, and sabotage the political situation of stability and unity. . . . If we tolerate or connive with this disturbance and let it go unchecked, a chaotic state will result. . . . A China with good prospects and a very bright future will become a chaotic and unstable China without any future."

The Communist Party has managed to put together fewer than twenty consecutive years of stability and growing prosperity. The dramatic and unprecedented nature of that growing prosperity makes it, in itself, somewhat chaotic and pregnant with unpredictable consequences. Moreover, this brief period of political stability and territorial integrity comes after generations of internal weakness and external interference, a situation with echoes of similar catastrophes that have afflicted the country repeatedly for thousands of years.

Understanding China's fear of chaos and disunity is a key to understanding policies and behaviour that are otherwise baffling for those who know little of Asian history. It helps to explain the atavistic impulse toward authoritarian rigidity by those who govern China, and it helps to explain China's conduct in international affairs. A country that can seem prickly, obstructive, stubborn, and insecure, ever ready to perceive insults to its sovereignty and dignity, becomes more readily understandable when seen through the prism of centuries of perceived humiliation. China's shrill reaction to Western leaders who meet with the exiled Tibetan spiritual leader, the Dalai Lama, for example, or to the most minuscule change in wording in any document relating to Taiwan, express more than a determination to stand firm on territorial positions not necessarily shared by everyone in the West. They also reflect the pain and shame of past weakness.

When the Soviet Union was collapsing in 1991, it was surprising at first to see extensive coverage of the crisis on Chinese television and in the newspapers. The hard-liners's *coup d'état*, the counter-coup led by Soviet Premier Boris Yeltsin from the turret of a tank, the mobs attacking Communist Party headquarters and the party newspaper *Pravda*, declarations of independence by Soviet republics, and the fall of Yeltsin's predecessor, Mikhail Gorbachev, were reported accurately and in detail.

At first, I thought it odd that the failure of communism in the USSR should be dealt with so openly and frankly by propaganda outlets usually given to covering up bad news. But then I understood the real message implicit in all those photographs from Moscow of tanks in the streets and mobs pulling down the hammer-and-sickle symbol from buildings. The message was: "See what happens when the party loses control! Chaos! It won't happen here."

As communism evaporated in the place where it all began, the *People's Daily* reported: "Socialism will replace Capitalism. Athough the road is winding and the struggle is fierce, the future is without doubt glorious and bright." And the government spokesman Yuan Mu told me, "No matter what happens in the Soviet Union, or in the whole international situation, the Chinese people will continue firmly and unshakably along the path they have chosen."

· 3 ·

DICTATORSHIP

"This is tyranny's disease: to trust no friend."

— AESCHYLUS

The crowd inched its way toward the presidential palace, nuns leading the way, their determined faces lit by the candles they were carrying. Every now and then shots were fired, but it was hard to tell where they were coming from. People would panic for a moment and scatter, crowding forward, pushing back, and then calm down and regroup. Those who had been toppled into the wide ditches by the side of the road clambered out, lucky not to have been trampled. When shots came from up ahead, the nuns would stop for a few minutes. They would pray and sing, then start walking again, slowly drawing the crowd behind them toward the palace.

As we reached the palace gates, ever more tightly packed together with people pushing from behind, we heard the sound of a helicopter taking off. Someone shouted that the president was gone and that the marines manning the machine-gun nests at the gates would not open fire. Suddenly we were scrambling over the wall. The people in front rushed the stairs to the upper floors, flung open the windows, and hurled out files. Presidential papers fluttered down over our heads as we stormed into the palace and found what was to become the world's most famous shoe collection.

I was laughing hysterically as I climbed over the wall. It was February 25, 1986, and I was still drunk from the long flight from London to Manila. I had landed just a few hours before an American helicopter airlifted Ferdinand and Imelda Marcos from the Malacanang Palace.

A few weeks previously, at the annual meeting of foreign correspondents at network headquarters, I had had a couple of bad scares. By this time, I always drank in the morning, and I was having frequent blackouts, sometimes even when I was not obviously drunk. It was like falling into a black hole. Later, I suddenly would become aware of my surroundings, but have no sense of how I came to be there, or what I had been doing for the previous hour or two. At the end of every year, correspondents from around the world would take part in a televised forum to review the news of the year in front of a live audience. During the taping of the 1985 year-end show, I came out of a blackout to find myself sitting on a stage in a crowded auditorium. For a few seconds I had no notion of where I was. Fortunately, someone else was talking, and I had minute or two to work out what was happening. It was not until I saw the recording later that I found out what questions I had been asked and how I had answered them. I was shaken up by the experience, but I put it down to jet-lag and overindulgence during the holidays. No one else was aware of what had happened, but my bosses did bring up the issue of my drinking in a private meeting soon after. I told them that I had sought medical advice, and was taking medication to bring the problem under control, which was a complete fabrication. Alcoholics make endless excuses and tell endless lies, to themselves as much as to others, but the on-air blackout and my managers' expression of concern made an impression. They were still on my mind a few weeks later when I travelled to the Philippines.

I resolved to control my drinking, of course, but found myself absolutely powerless to act on the resolution. To wake up in the morning was to experience a sudden jolt into consciousness, fear, and confusion. In a world made of broken glass, the only way to smooth the jagged edges was to take a drink. It was a reflex as strong as the one that compelled me to take the next breath. In the mornings, my preference was for vodka and orange juice, as a concession to the notion of a suitable breakfast, but I would drink whatever was available. Usually, I would throw up after the first few swallows, then persevere until I managed to keep a few ounces down. Even after going through this routine day after day for three years, I was able to delude myself that this was merely a phase brought about by whatever combination of circumstances I was dealing with at the time, and that one day soon things would go back to the way they used to be. In reality, I was living under a personal dictatorship as ruthless and difficult to overthrow as any of the regimes I was covering.

In February 1986, the four days of street protest known as "People Power" ended twenty-one years of dictatorship in the Philippines, but the regime had really begun to unravel the year before. Ferdinand and Imelda Marcos had become an embarrassment to their patrons in Washington, and under American pressure, they had agreed to hold a presidential election. They allowed the widow of one of Marcos's murdered critics to stand as a candidate. It was Marcos's intention to remain in office by rigging the election and claiming a popular mandate.

Ferdinand Marcos was a clever lawyer and politician who had been elected president in 1965. Imelda, a former beauty queen who liked to be known as "Mother of the Nation," combined the best qualities of Marie Antoinette and Miss Piggy from the *The Muppet Show*. They had prolonged their regime by declaring martial law in

1972, after a series of bombings in Manila that were attributed to the communist New People's Army (NPA) and the interception of a ship carrying weapons from China for the NPA. Marcos warned that, without martial law, "you will have communists going back and forth causing the dastardly ruin of our country, the killing of people, and the rape of women."

Ferdinand and Imelda were a greedy and murderous couple, backed by a corrupt and ruthless military and security apparatus. Marcos was the kind of right-wing strongman successive American presidents were comfortable with. "We love you, sir, we love your adherence to democratic principles," said Vice-President George H. W. Bush during a visit to Manila in 1981.

The candidate who stood against them, Corazon "Cory" Aquino, was an improbable revolutionary. A rather uninspiring member of an enormously wealthy and powerful family, she became opposition leader by default, when her husband, Benigno Aquino, Jr., was gunned down in 1983 at Manila International Airport. He had flown home after three years in exile, intending to build the opposition movement that his widow now inherited.

The Marcos's attempt to defuse the growing unrest by holding an election and allowing Aquino to run against them backfired badly. On February 15, the National Assembly, dominated by Marcos supporters, announced that Marcos had won. The opposition accused the election commission of fraud and claimed victory for Cory Aquino. The revolution began when the defence minister, Juan Ponce Enrile, and the deputy chief of staff of the armed forces, General Fidel V. Ramos, took Aquino's side. They formally renounced their support for Marcos and holed up in two military camps opposite each other on one of Manila's main boulevards, Epifanio de los Santos (EDSA). They were supported by about three hundred of the armed forces' 250,000 troops. Expecting an attack at any moment, Enrile requested assistance from Cardinal Jaime

Sin, the head of the Roman Catholic Church in the Philippines.

Cardinal Sin was already a vocal critic of the regime. Imelda had called him a "communist homosexual" after he criticized one of her pet projects, the Manila Film festival, as a "river of pornography and filth." He also joked that a picture of him standing between the president and the first lady made him "feel like Jesus, crucified between two thieves." Ignoring the Vatican's view that the Church should not intervene in politics, he took to the airwaves on the only non-government radio station, Radio Veritas, urging people to head for EDSA to form a human barricade around the rebel soldiers in Camp Crame and Camp Aguinaldo.

Next, the supporters of Aquino managed to capture a TV station, Channel Four, and began broadcasting telephone calls from people on the street reporting troop movements. They called for People Power reinforcements, mobilized Kiwanis clubs and medical students, appealed for volunteers to deliver cigarettes and toothpaste to the camp gates, and acted as a community bulletin board. Appeals for unarmed civilians to stand up to columns of troops were mingled with personal messages about who was going to be late home for dinner, who had got lost, who would be waiting at the usual place after work. When I checked into the Manila Hotel, four days into this revolution by telethon, every TV set was tuned to Channel Four, and that's how I learned that the presidential palace was the place to be. I had a quick drink and headed out.

While Channel Four was supporting the revolution, Channel Nine was still in the hands of the government. The line between politics and show business is especially blurred in the Philippines, and Marcos felt he needed to put on his own show. The day before his departure, he and the head of the armed forces, General Fabian Ver, were on television discussing what to do about the confrontations between the vast crowds of civilians and the army units ordered to disperse them. General Ver said the troops should open fire, but Marcos refused.

Marcos: "My order is not to attack."

Ver: "They are massing civilians near our troops, and we cannot keep withdrawing."

Marcos (interrupting): "My order is to disperse without shooting them."

Ver: "We cannot withdraw all the time."

Marcos: "No! No! No! Hold on! You disperse this crowd without shooting them."

It was an odd piece of grandstanding, and Marcos could easily have changed his mind, or given orders in private that were different from the ones he gave in front of the cameras. In the end, he did not use lethal force to preserve his regime, but instead took an American offer of a helicopter ride to Hawaii, where he died in exile in 1989.

The Filipinos had won back their democracy, but they then proceeded to squander what they had won. In 1986 and 1987, I went back often to cover coup attempts and other crises of one kind and another. During this time, my behaviour became increasingly erratic. On one trip, I was supposed to be making clandestine contact with the New People's Army to report on the continuing communist insurgency. I got as far as the address of a contact who would arrange the trip. It was a coffin-maker's workshop in a village outside Manila. We arrived late at night, and as we sat among the rows of coffins, I tried to make a joke about the suitability of a funeral business as a front for the NPA, which was famous for its assassination teams known as "sparrow squads." "Economic integration!" I slurred. The people we had come to meet quietly asked me to leave. The trip was off.

Another night, I persuaded my local assistant that we needed to go out to buy a handgun. If I had been sober, I could easily have accomplished the errand in a place like Manila, but I would never have wanted to, and have never wanted to before or since. Because I was drunk, and wrapped up in a fantasy of being like the gonzo journalist Hunter S. Thompson, I wanted a Browning 9-mm pistol to take back to Britain. I was fortunate to be dismissed as a fool by my assistant before I bought one and tried to smuggle it home. Not so fortunately, my assistant resigned because he did not want to be involved with such a dangerous idiot. A few days later, when I returned to London, I was hospitalized for a week. I had gone to see my doctor because I had lost colour vision. My liver-function tests were dangerously abnormal, but he diagnosed exhaustion rather than alcoholism, because I had always lied to him about the amount I drank. He was surprised when, a few months later, I asked him to find a treatment centre, after I was told by my employers either to go into treatment or find another employer. Many doctors are strangely blind to alcoholism, and we alcoholics can be very convincing liars. My doctor was one of the very few people who in those days did not know or suspect that I was a problem drinker.

Filipinos like to describe their history as "four hundred years in the convent, and fifty years in Hollywood." Colonization first by Spain and then by the United States has had bizarre results. The political system is a carnival mix of feudalism, show business, religion, and organized crime. Elections are noisy caricatures of democracy in which voters choose from a broad roster of shallow, silly, and venal candidates. These campaigns are enormously amusing, but they give the impression that the right to choose stupid politicians for stupid reasons trumps all the other rights that democracy is supposed to offer to citizens.

Cory Aquino's disappointing presidency was followed by the relatively effective one of Fidel Ramos. He had been one of the key players in the 1986 revolution. Now he gave up his military uniform for a politician's suit, and became president in 1992. By that time, five years had passed since my last drink, and I found that covering Filipino politics sober was almost as strange as doing it drunk. Imelda Marcos had not only been allowed to return home in 1991, but she also was running for president. I followed her around for a couple of days, flabbergasted both by her sociopathic self-absorption and by her continuing appeal to millions of voters. She explained her legendary extravagance in terms of her duty to set an example for the poor: "You have to be some kind of light, a star to give them guidelines." She might have won if the vote for the myth of the Marcos years as a golden age had not been split between her and Eduardo Cohuangco, Jr., an ambitious former Marcos crony. Between them, they garnered more than six million votes. Fidel Ramos won with just over five million.

Ramos revived the country's economy, then distinguished himself further by resisting the temptation to engineer a constitutional change that would allow him to seek a second term of office. It was tempting to think that the electorate and the elected both had been struck sensible, but the 1998 election proved that this was not the case.

Imelda ran again, but realized early on she was not going to win. She threw her support behind the eventual winner, Joseph Estrada, a loutish clown who had been the star of more than a hundred dreadful films, and who had once been thrown out of college for "repugnant conduct." His campaign train was a travelling circus of cronies, political hacks, soap-opera stars, pop singers, and hangers-on, and so was his administration after he won. In that sense, no one could say that Estrada was dishonest — what the voters saw was what the voters got. He did not try to conceal his promiscuity, his drinking, and his loyalty to unsavoury acquaintances. He admitted to everything with a boyish smirk that suggested he was a lovable rogue who should be forgiven for having a few weaknesses.

Watching him was sometimes like looking into the mirror of my own past. People were not really voting for Estrada, the man. They were voting for the working-class hero he played in his movies, a tough guy with a heart of gold, who stood up for the downtrodden.

In 2000, after two years in office and with four to go, President Estrada was hitting his stride when it all fell apart. He was in the habit of staying up into the early hours, drinking and playing high-stakes mah-jong with a cabal of crooked businessmen. This became known as the "Midnight Cabinet" because of the numerous presidential decisions that emerged from its sessions. One of the participants was Luis Singson, governor of Ilocos Sur, a province known as "Warlord Country" because guns, goons, and gambling reigned supreme. One of Singson's rackets was *jueteng*, a nationwide, illegal lottery. He shared the profits with the president, who needed money for the five mistresses he had installed in expensive mansions around Manila.

Estrada realized that he could raise even more money by creating a legal lottery. All might have been well if his plans had included his old friend Luis who, after all, had been regularly delivering him briefcases full of cash. Instead, Estrada gave the licence for the new game, Bingo 2-ball, to one of Singson's rivals. Singson, understandably upset, went public.

"All I wanted was the Bingo 2-ball," he said, explaining why he became a whistle-blower. "But they gave the licence to my bitter opponent."

Armed with Singson's revelations and other allegations of corruption, the Congress impeached the president, forcing the Senate to begin a trial. I arrived in Manila on January 17, 2001, the day a majority of senators, who fed in the same corrupt swamp as Estrada, voted not to examine key pieces of evidence. This vote set off the revolution known as EDSA II.

EDSA II was called a second People Power revolution, but really it was a revolution by only some of the people — the elite and the middle class — who seemed to be offended as much by Estrada's vulgarity as by his criminality. The less educated and less well-off still adored Estrada, and thought the muckety-mucks were trying to steal the presidency. There was considerable tension in the days of demonstrations and counter-demonstrations. And, just as in the first revolution fourteen years earlier, the armed forces made the difference.

The site of the 1986 demonstrations on EDSA had become a shrine, and was an obvious rallying point for the anti-Estrada movement, once the Senate had shown that the trial would be rigged. After three days of singing, chanting, and speech-making, it was announced that key military figures were withdrawing support from Estrada. He was holed up in the palace getting drunker and drunker as the days went by. This time, no one stormed the presidential palace. We reporters were crammed onto the stage at the EDSA shrine with the cream of Manila society, including Cardinal Sin, army generals, former presidents, senators, congressmen, the usual crowd of hangers-on, and choirs of nuns, to witness the chief justice of the Supreme Court swear in Vice-President Gloria Macapagal Arroyo as acting president. Estrada, stumbling drunkenly, was escorted out the back door of the palace and taken away by boat, saying he was stepping down temporarily to avoid bloodshed. Estrada never signed a resignation document, and the Senate never convicted him. There was no legal, constitutional, or democratic basis whatever for the way he was ousted. The Supreme Court simply got on the bandwagon, declared the presidency vacant, and swore in a successor.

Estrada was not a strongman; he was weak and foolish. Still, he faced the same moment of decision that Marcos had faced, isolated in the Malacanang Palace, unable to depend on the armed forces to suppress the revolt raging on the streets outside. I have always wanted to be in the room to witness the dictator's dilemma, the moment when he decides whether to fight or to go. Dictators need a combination of supreme confidence and fundamental insecurity to wriggle up to the top of the heap and then quash all rivals. After all those years of imagining what threats there may be, what plots might be hatched, and moving to pre-empt them, what is it that makes such a person decide that the jig is up? The key factor, I believe, is the loyalty of the security apparatus. As long as the army, police, and spies are willing to shoot in defence of the regime, People Power is generally hopeless. It is the regime, however, that becomes hopeless when the armed forces change sides, start fighting among themselves, or sit on their hands. The Shah of Iran lost when the army would not control demands on the street for the Ayatollah's return. Marcos lost when General Fidel Ramos ordered his troops to protect the protestors who had taken over Channel Four.

I was delighted to be on hand when that moment of decision came for Indonesia's strongman, Haji Muhammad Suharto, in 1998. After thirty-two years in power, he was the last of Asia's classic right-wing dictators. And for most of those thirty-two years, he was surprisingly immune from the sort of criticism usually directed at one-man rule.

Suharto's regime came complete with a bogus parliament elected by huge majorities in rigged elections, fawning official media, and thought-police to guard the legacy of the Great Man's theories and philosophy, known as *pancasila*. Multinational corporations found the Suharto regime easy to deal with. All they had to do was pick a partner from the list of untouchable family members and friends, and take advantage of Indonesia's wealth of natural resources and a seemingly disciplined and docile workforce. That America supported an anti-communist strongman, holding together a huge archipelago of 13,000 islands and a population of more than two hundred million people, was no surprise. During the Vietnam War, any Asian thug who could claim to be keeping his particular domino upright was sure of unquestioned American support.

It is less easy to understand why countries like Australia, Canada, Germany, and Britain were equally keen to overlook the regime's shortcomings and to be seduced by Indonesia's apparent economic miracle. It was convenient to believe that Indonesians welcomed Suharto's rule as a guarantee of stability and economic progress, and saw the lack of political freedom as a reasonable price to pay for a steady improvement in living standards. It was convenient to ignore the fact that the army and secret police locked up Suharto's opponents, real or imagined, or simply made them disappear.

It was the Asian economic meltdown of 1997 that laid the groundwork for Suharto's downfall. Indonesia's currency, the rupiah, collapsed and almost everyone's personal finances collapsed with it. Fifteen million people were pushed below the poverty line overnight. Resentment over the shameless plunder of the economy by Suharto's family and friends became sharper than ever.

Suharto's multi-billionaire children had grabbed chunks of every conceivable business: mining, power generation, toll roads, an airline, plastics, timber, paper, construction, fisheries, food processing, broadcasting, banking, newspapers, shipping, real estate, plantations, car manufacturing, and taxis, to name just a few. They often were in partnership with favoured Chinese-Indonesian business interests that controlled three-quarters of the 140 biggest conglomerates. Although much of his wealth depended on those partnerships, Suharto had not been shy of instigating anti-Chinese pogroms when it suited him. A dictator who claims credit for everything usually has to have someone to blame when things turn sour. In the European tradition, fingers are pointed at mysterious foreign forces, international financiers, or a worldwide conspiracy of Freemasons and Jews. In Indonesia, the Chinese are the scapegoats.

Since 1996, when opposition to Suharto started to become more evident, political ferment coalesced around Megawati Sukarnoputri, the daughter of Indonesia's first president. The economic meltdown gave impetus to a growing protest movement among students, but despite the unpopular measures taken under pressure from the International Monetary Fund, and despite widespread public dissatisfaction, the Suharto regime was weathering the storm reasonably well. There was no united opposition movement. There was no institution with organizational and moral power comparable to the Catholic Church in both Poland and the Philippines. And there was no obvious disloyalty within the armed services. A year into the Asian financial crisis, there was little sign of a constellation of conditions that might be sufficient to topple Suharto.

It is not clear exactly who did what during the nine days in May 1998 that brought Suharto down. Indonesians believe Suharto's son-in-law, General Prabowo Subianto, who was married to Suharto's third daughter Titiek, played a key role. At the time, Prabowo was in command of the strategic reserve, the Komando Strategis Cadangan Angkatan Darat (KOSTRAD). Earlier he had commanded the special forces, Komando Pasukan Khusus (KOPASSUS), known to be responsible for the kidnapping, torture, and murder of many suspected opponents of the regime. Paramilitary militias sponsored by KOPASSUS were often commanded by serving or retired military officers. They were responsible for many violent operations on behalf of the official security apparatus, eliminating troublesome individuals or organizations, and committing atrocities that were used as a pretext for repressive measures. Prabowo denies responsibility for the disaster of May

1998, but it seems highly likely that it was his hubris and stupidity that precipitated his father-in-law's fall.

It started on May 12. Student demonstrations had become relatively commonplace, and so long as they did not leave the university campus, little was done to suppress them. This time, students planning a march to parliament were in a standoff with police at the gates of the elite Trisakti University for most of the day when, late in the afternoon, shots were fired, killing four students. Eyewitnesses said they saw men on motorcycles stop on the overpass overlooking the gate and open fire. It was later determined that the bullet recovered from the body of one of the dead students was fired by a rifle issued only to the military, not to the police. At the time, the incident seemed unlike anything that had happened before. The shots appeared not to have been fired as a crowd control measure. Rather, it seemed that the students had been picked off by professional snipers, with the aim of escalating tensions and providing a context for further planned violence.

The students and many middle-class Indonesians were outraged by the Trisakti killings. This was the first time students had been killed in two years of anti-Suharto activity. Thousands attended a memorial service at the university the next morning, and an angry crowd gathered at the university gates. Many students said they had no intention of obeying the unwritten rule that they stay on campus, but as the mob outside the gates turned ugly, most students withdrew. Cars were set on fire, and violence quickly spread through the city.

Reports that Jakarta was in flames were enough to get me moving from my home in Bangkok. I travelled as a tourist because a journalist's visa was impossible to obtain on such short notice.

As my plane came in to land, I could see plumes of dark smoke rising from the Glodok district near the old city in the north end of Jakarta. The one statistic every Indonesian knows is that ethnic

Chinese account for about 3 percent of the population of the country, but control 70 percent of the wealth. In Jakarta, as in many cities, there's a large concentration of Chinese businesses and homes in one particular district. Jakarta's Chinatown, Glodok, was in flames.

Months before, Indonesian special forces had rappelled from helicopters into Glodok, supposedly to show how they would protect the Chinese community if necessary, but actually to remind everyone how vulnerable that community was. When Glodok and other parts of the city came under attack, neither police nor troops were deployed to protect them. Those in uniform on the edges of Glodok allowed the mobs to pass through on their murderous mission, while soldiers out of uniform organized the mobs and egged them on, as well as raping, killing, and setting fires themselves. A report prepared by Indonesia's Human Rights Commission quotes eyewitnesses who described many participants in what became three days of horrors as "well-built with short cropped hair." Many of the charred corpses laid out in the morgues belonged to looters trapped when the malls they were pillaging were set on fire. Mobs cheered as Chinese women were pulled from cars, stripped, raped, and in some cases burned alive. Other Chinese women were raped and killed in their homes or businesses.

Still, even after Suharto was overthrown, the Human Rights Commission report was cautious about blaming the military. It said the trouble was instigated and directed by "certain groups" — code for units of the Indonesian armed forces it was not safe to name. There is no doubt that the violent events that brought Suharto down were different from the spontaneous violence and chaos that can occur in the dying days of a long dictatorship. They were planned acts of wickedness, intended to manipulate events.

Suharto was on an official visit to Cairo when the Trisakti students were shot. It is generally supposed in Jakarta that Prabowo's motive in inciting unrest in the capital was to prove that the minister of defence and security, General Wiranto, was unable to control the situation. He then would be replaced by Prabowo, who would quickly restore order. The riots would provide the pretext for a declaration of martial law and Prabowo, having stepped into Wiranto's shoes, would in due course step into his father-in law's. One persuasive argument that this was indeed the plan is its similarity to the way Suharto came to power back in 1966. He intervened after an abortive coup supposedly engineered by the Communist Party against his predecessor Sukarno. As many as half a million people were killed as he consolidated his power, with a purge against communists, coupled with a pogrom against the Chinese.

As Chinese were again being murdered in the Indonesian capital, Suharto rushed home. The violence died down when army units not controlled by Prabowo or his allies were finally deployed. There was a short lull before the next phase, which did not follow the script. Foreigners and Indonesian Chinese were fleeing the country in large numbers, international reaction was scathing, and there was enormous damage to an economy that was already crippled. Individuals and groups that had previously supported Suharto started to desert him. Wiranto and Prabowo jointly pledged support for the president, but their rivalry was now out in the open. Prabowo was not strong enough to push Wiranto aside.

Instead of consolidating and prolonging the regime, Prabowo's dark schemes had produced a coherent national opposition united behind a common goal — the ousting of Suharto — and military forces divided in their willingness to kill to keep the opposition out.

Jakarta is a spread-out city with wide boulevards that are hard for pedestrians to cross but easy to march along. When there were big rallies or protests, the long distances between different areas of the city made it difficult to get around on foot, and a car was inconvenient because traffic became impossible. The only way to cover the upheavals before and after Suharto's departure was to buzz around the city on the back of a small motorcycle. I consider myself lucky to have lived through the experience.

The regime change in Indonesia was the first major story to be reported from a place where cellphones had come into widespread use. After losing two or three to the newly poor Indonesians who had turned to petty theft, I bought a dog leash and wore my phone chained to my belt. For the first time, we journalists could call around and quickly find out what was going on in other parts of the city. We could also call in on-the-spot radio reports anytime, anywhere. As with any revolutionary technology, it is hard now to imagine how we had ever managed without it.

Indonesian soldiers mostly had orders to avoid killing foreign journalists, so it was quite easy to move around, seeking vantage points either on the protestors' side or with the soldiers. The feeling of invulnerability was rather like wearing an invisibility cloak, but it could be dangerous. Once, when the mayhem continued after dark, it did not occur to me that the soldiers, who were firing live ammunition, would no longer be able to distinguish between foreigners and protestors. After visiting a hospital, and counting the wounded who were arriving at a rate of one every six minutes, I wandered out into the street leading back to the hotel. Suddenly, I saw a muzzle flash and narrowly missed being cut down by a burst of automatic fire that splatted against the building beside me. One of the most dangerous aspects of dangerous places is that you get used to them very quickly and drop your guard.

On May 19, 1998, students occupied the parliament buildings and demanded that Suharto step down. As soon as I learned of this development, I slipped through a military cordon on the back of a motorcycle and climbed over a fence to join them.

The mood at the parliament was like the mood in Tiananmen Square in 1989. An army of flag-waving students, reinforced by support from the general population, was refusing to budge.

Suharto made a feeble attempt to bring the crisis to a close in a televised speech in which he promised new elections in which he would not be a candidate. It was not a deal anyone was willing to accept. Opposition forces announced a gigantic march for May 20, then called it off when the army deployed thousands of troops and armoured vehicles to stop them. At the same time, Wiranto told Suharto that he no longer had the support of the army.

At nine o'clock on May 21, Suharto was back on television reading his resignation speech. As in the Philippines, people had been willing to risk getting shot, but the military was unwilling to shoot them.

———————

ZHANG QINGYI WAS THIRTEEN years old when he joined China's revolution to fight the worst dictator of all — hunger. "In Sichuan at the time we were very poor," he says. "There wasn't enough to eat. I joined in 1933. In 1935, when I was fifteen, we began the Long March."

Zhang Qingyi was a short man with a wiry grey brush cut and the ramrod-straight back of a proud old soldier. He was sitting outside his home, a cave carved out of a yellow-brown hillside in Shaanxi Province, when I met him in 1993.

He lives close to Yanan, the final destination of the Long March — the communists' legendary, year-long retreat from one end of China to the other. The Long March enabled the three communist armies to escape encirclement by the Guomindang, the opposing nationalists, and it enabled Mao Zedong to consolidate his position as unchallenged leader of the Communist Party. Yanan was a safe base, with close access to Soviet support for the war against the Guomindang and the Japanese occupation.

As a veteran of the Long March, Zhang is a member of China's revolutionary aristocracy. He feels he has earned the right to speak his mind about what the Communist Party has done with the country he fought for. "When the Red Army came to Sichuan, they said they would smash the landlords and share out the land. Because our family was very poor, we came out to join up," he told me. "I was only thirteen and they didn't want me at first. I ran along behind them for more than a month before they finally let me join. It was quite a process."

Zhang Qingyi is a cave-dweller, but his life is not quite the primitive Cro-Magnon existence the term conjures up. Warm in winter, cool in summer, the cave is about seventy square metres in extent, with arched ceilings. From the outside, it looks like the mouth of a railway tunnel blocked off by a brick front. Its door and windows match the colour of the broad hills and valleys of this dusty landscape. Caves like this are home to more than forty million Chinese.

. Although Mao Zedong is still Zhang Qingyi's hero, he thinks Mao's perpetual political campaigns ruined the economy. "If ordinary people don't have a decent life, what kind of communism is that? What kind of socialism is that?" Zhang said to me, wagging his finger sternly. He believes his old commander, Deng Xiaoping, was right to introduce economic reforms after Mao's death.

"When I served under Deng, we all thought he was very clever, but we never imagined he could become a great national leader. What he did, reform and opening up, was absolutely right." But, Zhang says, corruption and greed are betraying the ideals he fought for. "In the old days, all we thought about was serving the people and doing a good job," he said. "Now people put millions in their pockets. They are ruining the country, ruining socialism, and bringing moral ruin on themselves.

"The problem is with local officials," Zhang continued, growing angry. "The central government doesn't control them strictly enough, and people in the legal system are on the take, too." He quotes an old proverb that says the reason a judge's hat curves up on both sides of his head is so that he can profit from both sides in a case.

"Officials make up their own rules. Corruption is like a hammer smashing everything. We have to be opposed to this. How can we not be against it?"

If an elderly cave-dweller who never went to school can diagnose the central problem of governance in China, and if he quotes proverbs more than two thousand years old to make his point, it's not surprising that the government should also be able to identify the problem. At the annual meeting of the National People's Congress, China's parliament, it is now routine for the premier to state that corruption is a problem, that the future of the country and the Communist Party depend on tackling it, and that anti-corruption efforts will intensify in the coming year.

"As regards the corrupt elements, no matter where they are, who are involved, and how high-ranking their positions are, we must severely punish and deal with them in accordance with the law," said Premier Wen Jiabao in a typical speech in 2005. He went on to outline a set of qualifications for those who hold public office:

> It is imperative to build a contingent of public servants who are politically reliable, professionally competent, and clean and honest and have a good working style. They should emancipate their minds, seek truth from facts, and keep pace with the times . . . abide by the Constitution and the law . . . be dedicated, hard-working, and eager to learn . . . observe disciplinary regulations and professional ethics . . . be honest, clean, upright, impartial, and devoted . . . remain modest and prudent, guard against an arrogant and rash working style, and continue to live plainly and work hard.

Chinese leaders have been saying the same thing since Confucius.

No one is surprised anymore by the billions of dollars the top leaders' families have acquired in the transition from Marx to the Market, nor the countless millions that mayors and provincial governors rake in. Nobody finds it a mystery that a minister on an official salary of a few thousand yuan a month can afford to educate his children at Harrow or Harvard, and everyone knows that underpaid doctors cheat their patients by prescribing unneeded drugs. All of this is simple theft. Granted, it's theft on a grand scale that disgraces every single person in an official position, including those who are honest themselves yet turn a blind eye to those who are not, but it's no different from what happens wherever people have itchy fingers and think no one can stop them from taking what they want.

Ordinary people in China — known as *laobaixing*, "the old one hundred names" — are not entirely shocked by the corrupt enrichment endemic among Chinese officials. Many feel this is inevitable, and that they might do the same if they could. What does outrage *laobaixing* is injustice. Take, for example, the case of Zhang Yuchen. This wealthy businessman has the absurd bouffant hairstyle favoured by Chinese men who wish they were taller and the self-satisfied smirk that comes from owning a $50-million chateau. He held a senior position in the Beijing Construction Bureau until 1992, when he "jumped into the sea," slang for leaving a government job to go into business.

"Jumping into the sea" typically involves using your official position to accumulate capital by doing favours for private business people who need your approval for projects, then quitting your job to go into business with some of those same people, while continuing to feed and water your former colleagues in government offices whose approval *you* now need for your projects. A truly successful plunge includes making sure that companies controlled by you, your family, and friends wind up as owners of the prime real estate that used to belong to one of the dying state industries you were involved with as a government official.

When I met Zhang Yuchen, he declined to share exact details of his business dealings in the ten years he's been swimming. He admits that his connections were very important in the early 1990s, but says things have changed: "I think that now China is gradually becoming more regulated. Connections are definitely useful, but they are not of major importance now that land is auctioned off on the open market. It's impossible now to get land through connections. You have to compete."

Zhang Yuchen's pride and joy is an exact replica of the Château Maisons-Lafitte on the outskirts of Beijing. It is a hotel, and the centrepiece of a development of million-dollar villas. The original, on the river Seine in France, was owned by the Comte d'Artois, brother of King Louis XVI. In his day, the count's ostentatious extravagance made him almost as unpopular as his great friend Marie Antoinette.

Zhang is the archetype of China's nouveaux riches, known as *baofahu*, or "explosively wealthy households." Believing himself to be a connoisseur of fine architecture, he attached a replica of part of the coliseum in Rome to his seventeenth-century château because, he says, "It looks splendid."

After he boasts of his collection of Château Lafite Rothschild wines worth thousands of dollars a bottle, and the cost of the golden Chantilly stone imported from France, Zhang tells me that the people who used to farm the land are glad of the opportunity to work at the château. "I think most of them are satisfied," he said. "That's not to say 100 percent, but most."

After leaving Zhang, I came across an old couple peering through the padlocked back gate of the château grounds at the landscapers working on the rolling lawn where their tiny farm used to be. "There's not one finger of land left, it all belongs to the castle," said Wu Shurui, rattling the gate. "The whole village was sold."

"They told us the villagers would be shareholders," said his wife, Li Xiulan. "We don't understand this policy at all. We peasants don't have a penny now. How can we be called shareholders?"

"In 1949, the Communist Party gave each family five *mu* of land. It was the first time we ever had any land to call our own," said Wu. Five *mu* is about one-third of a hectare. Thousands of hectares were expropriated for Zhang Yuchen's château.

"We have supported the Communist Party all our lives. Now we're landless again. We have no money, and they say we are shareholders!" said Li. As they walked away from the gates back to their two-room home, they continued grumbling. Of course, economic reform has made some people rich, they said, but that's no reason to leave ordinary people with nothing. All they want is a fair deal. "If the state were to take the land, that's no problem, we have no objection at all, but this is for capitalist entertainment!"

Around the time Zhang Yuchen was jumping into the sea in the early 1990s, I went with a friend to visit a pair of elderly aunts, who were about to lose their family home. Most of the old courtyard homes in their neighbourhood in the heart of old Beijing were already rubble, but the Fan sisters, in their seventies, had held out as long as they could. The water and electricity were about to be cut off, and as we talked, the noise of jackhammers was deafening.

Fan Qi, a silver-haired butterball of a woman, said she loved the neighbourhood where the sisters had lived all their lives, but they couldn't stay any longer. "It's like an earthquake, with the walls shaking," she said. "We have to move to the apartment they have offered us."

Her bird-like sister, Fan Shan, remembered the days when their wealthy father would bring home Beijing Opera stars for a private performance. She loves to sing and felt the only good thing about the situation was that now that the neighbours had moved out, she could let rip without worrying about complaints. Luckily, her sister likes to listen. "I won't be able to sing when we're in an apartment. We don't want to live in a high-rise, but we have no choice," she told me. The land their house sat on in the centre of town was far more valuable than an apartment out in the suburbs. Fan Shan lowered her voice a little, looking over her shoulder as if someone might be listening, when she said government and Communist Party officials, whom she referred to with a dismissive nod as "*they*," were in cahoots with the developers to make a fortune. "*They* never even say whether we have a right to refuse to leave, whether we have any legal protection," she said.

"That's what I'm most unhappy about," said Fan Qi. "Isn't there supposed to be a law to protect us?" Still, when the time came the sisters moved out quietly.

Ten years later, people were not going so quietly. In 2005, the minister of public security, Zhou Yongkang, reported that the number of "mass incidents," code for protests, riots, and other disturbances, had risen from an annual figure of 10,000 in 1995 to 74,000. As is often the case in China, the figures are not completely reliable. Rather than reflecting what actually happened, statistics often are adjusted to suit the government's current agenda. What was significant, however, was that a government that used to portray China as a place where everyone was happy and nothing ever went wrong, now was admitting that there was a public disturbance somewhere in China a hundred times every day. The vast majority of these mass incidents result from the loss of land or homes without adequate compensation. In the countryside, farmland is grabbed by local officials, or by industrial concerns in league with local officials, to build factories, golf courses, or suburban housing developments. In the cities, whole neighbourhoods are demolished to make way for shopping centres and office towers. Many of these conflicts turn into riots because the police and courts are on the side of the winners, and the losers are angry and frustrated, and have nowhere to turn.

Hua Xinmin is a tireless campaigner for the preservation of Beijing's historic neighbourhoods. She is also fighting an epic legal battle to get back the property on which her grandfather, an engineer, built the family home in the early part of last century. Her father, an architect, was working in France when the People's Republic was founded in 1949. Like many Chinese intellectuals who were living overseas at the time, he came home to help build the new China. It was a time of great hope and promise, before Mao Zedong's ruinous political campaigns, and it was remembered with fondness by those who took part in the efforts to rebuild industry, education, health services, and everything else after years of war.

Then came the Cultural Revolution. The Hua family was thrown out on the street, and their house was given by Red Guards to families with a correct class background.

Hua Xinmin takes visitors to see the place where the home designed by her grandfather used to stand, a two-thousand-square-metre site not far from Tiananmen Square and the Forbidden City. The site, now occupied by the Beijing branch of the Hong Kong Jockey Club, is worth a large fortune. She has title deeds going back to the Qing Dynasty, as well as a deed issued by the People's Republic in 1951 confirming the Hua family's ownership. "The only compensation given to anyone was given to the people who were assigned to live in our house when we were thown out by the Red Guards during the Cultural Revolution. We got nothing," she said. The government bureau that is required by law to handle the restoration of property seized illegally during the Cultural Revolution has taken more than thirty years to consider the case. In the meantime, the department administering the site sold it to a developer, which demolished the Hua family home to build a luxurious clubhouse to lease to the club. "It may be corruption, or it may be something else. I don't know," said Hua Xinmin. "Many people are in this situation. Some get their property back, some don't. Some cities deal with it one way, others deal with it another way. There is one law, one government, and it should deal with everyone equally. There's nothing wrong with the law, it's the application of the law." Still, she is determined to win. "In principle the Jockey Club should be demolished," she said. "That may not happen, but at the very least we will have to be given compensation."

Another tireless campaigner for citizens' rights is Wu Qing. She is serving her seventh term on the district People's Congress, the local council. Once a week, Wu Qing holds office hours for her constituents in Haidian, Beijing's university district. Dozens of people clutching files and plastic bags full of documents line up outside, chatting as they wait their turn to see her. Every single one wants Wu Qing's help to right a wrong. The most common grievances concern expropriated property, unfair court judgements, and arbitrary and abusive official conduct. "People come here for help to fight exploitation and injustice," says Wu Qing. "There's not enough justice, and we have to fight every step of the way. When people's rights are being violated, they come here and say, 'Where are my rights?' They should know their rights *before* they are violated. People have to be educated, but now they're educating themselves because they have been exploited and maltreated."

Wu Qing has carved out a unique career in China as an independent and outspoken politician. She was first elected in the 1980s, after campaigning for a pedestrian bridge over a dangerous road near the Foreign Language University, where she was a professor for forty years. She is an indefatigable champion of women's rights and a powerful supporter of a network of non-governmental organizations working to improve the lot of women in rural China.

She radiates determination and energy. Her salt-and-pepper hair and her speech pattern share a short, no-nonsense style.

Her mother, Bing Xin, was a national icon. She was a great writer of novels and books for children. She also was a member of the May 4 student movement of 1919. The date marks an historic turning point recognized by both democrats and communists alike. Having such a famous mother has given Wu Qing the licence to be forthright, a freedom generally denied to those lacking such an impeccable pedigree, but she also judiciously avoids direct public criticism of the party or its leading members. She says out loud what many dare not say — that China should have freedom and democracy, albeit slowly.

"I've been through so many political movements. Especially the Cultural Revolution. I think enough is enough. We have to start something new," she says. "Of course, it will not be so new, because ever since the May 4 movement, students and intellectuals have been fighting for freedom and democracy. What we should start now is a new May 4 movement. We should have the rule of law, and people should be able to enjoy freedom and democracy."

Nonetheless, Wu Qing believes gradual change is best. She always carries a well-thumbed copy of the Chinese constitution, its cover stained by tea spilled in countless meetings with constituents. "I think the constitution is sacred. Every single citizen should know enough about the content to know their rights and responsibilities. Last year, the amendment guaranteeing respect and protection for human rights was added, as well as respect for private property. That's great progress. Once it's in the constitution, I can use it. We are not asking for more, just that those in power implement what's there. That's good enough."

I told Wu Qing about a demonstration I had seen a few days before, where merchants staged a noisy protest because their market was about to be demolished to make way for a new development with sky-high rents. One had said to me, "The developers are just businessmen like us, but they have officials on their side. How could a private businessman get all these police out like this?" Another shouted, "There's no democracy, they don't discuss things. They decide on demolition and just go right ahead. We have no freedom of speech. There should be democracy."

When police tried to stop my cameraman from filming the demonstration, the protestors came to our aid, shouting, "Press freedom! Press freedom!" I told Wu Qing that some of the protestors were waving copies of the constitution, and she almost bounced out of her chair with enthusiasm. "Little potatoes know more about the constitution and the law than people at the top," she said. "With modern technology, people know more, people move around more. In Beijing, we have five million migrants. There are so many people coming and going, taking information with them. There are new ways of thinking, new ways of doing things. No one can close the door any more, no one. Some local governments still try, but it's hard. People have cellphones and the Internet. Modern technology is playing a very important role. That's where the strength is. It's simmering up. I'm optimistic, but there is no way it can be smooth. There are zigs and zags, ups and downs. That's life."

Progress is slow, notes Wu Qing, especially in the countryside, where entrenched local leaders are used to getting their own way. "Progress will be a gradual thing, a new Long March. China has had 2,400 years of feudalism. Even since 1949, I think, in some ways feudalism has been reinforced. Rights are never given and granted. You have to fight every step of the way."

Chen Guangcheng, a thirty-four-year-old blind man, fought back in September 2005 when a gang of thugs grabbed him outside a Beijing apartment building and bundled him into a car. Passersby saw and heard the struggle, and intervened to prevent the car from leaving until the police came. When the thugs showed the Beijing policemen their Shandong Province police identity cards, however, the Beijing police cleared the good Samaritans out of the way of the car, and Chen Guangcheng was driven away.

Chen Guangcheng is a "barefoot lawyer," a new kind of activist named after the untrained "barefoot doctors" who brought medical care to remote villages in the early years of the People's Republic. Blind from birth, Chen found his vocation when he made a complaint in Beijing about the local taxes that were being levied against him despite a national law giving an exemption to the disabled. After he fought and won the case, he began studying the law and taking up cases for others. He extended his range from helping people with disabilities to taking on a factory that was pouring dangerous chemicals into a river and, finally, preparing a class-action lawsuit to stop the local authorities using forced abortions and sterilizations to meet family planning targets under the one-child policy.

Chen's David-and-Goliath victories won national and international attention. Stories were written about him in publications like *Newsweek* and the *Washington Post*, and he won funding for a four-week trip to the United States, where he learned about Western legal practices and theory, and met Jerome Cohen, the most distinguished Western authority on the law in China.

"Chen is a profoundly impressive person. He has a quiet charisma and keen intelligence, and he is an eloquent speaker," says Cohen, who has been involved with legal issues in China since 1972. Cohen's advice has been sought by countless senior Chinese officials, as well as by Western governments and companies. Although he now is in his late seventies, he still spends part of the year teaching law in the Chinese language in Chinese universities.

I usually pay attention to my mother's stern advice, "Never trust a man in a bow tie!" but in Jerome Cohen's case, I make an exception. He is an eloquent, courtly man who generously shares his deep understanding of China.

"Local officials are very unhappy when some of their people get legal knowledge, because they know that they're going to be challenged, and that's where a lot of social upsets come from — local people learning something about their rights, learning something about procedures, and trying to challenge abusive authority," says Cohen.

One unusual feature of Chinese law is that the role of *bian-huren,* or "defender," is not restricted to lawyers. Professional lawyers are often unwilling to get involved with defendants in controversial cases, political cases, or in cases that challenge an abuse of power. Courageous barefoot lawyers are filling a need. Chinese bookstores are surprisingly full of do-it-yourself books on the law and court procedure, and despite everything that has happened to Chen and others, it is an encouraging sign that more and more people are buying and using them.

"Lawyers in China today must be courageous, and yet they're under increasing pressure and restriction. Sometimes the government takes a lawyer's licence away, sometimes they are punished criminally for refusing to *stop* helping people. Lawyers are an endangered species," says Cohen.

Chen was going head-to-head with local leaders by travelling around the county, systematically gathering evidence of cases where family-planning officials had forced sterilization and abortions on people to meet quotas on which their own bonuses and promotions might depend. The practice of forced sterilization used to be widespread, but since the mid-1990s, official policy has been to implement a system of financial incentives for compliance, backed up by fines for non-compliance. Chen's evidence and his legal arguments were incontrovertible, and in September 2005 he had come to Beijing to persuade national officials to deal with abuses in Linyi. He had also come to meet foreign journalists. International publicity can sometimes help protect people who are challenging the authorities.

I had been talking to Chen Guangcheng on the phone for a few months before his Beijing visit. I was planning to go to Shandong to spend some time following him around in Linyi for a television profile. He called me when he arrived in Beijing, but since he already had a busy schedule, I said I did not need time for an interview, which would in any case be much better for our program if it were filmed on location in Linyi.

I did drop by to say hello during a meeting that he, and a couple of dozen other blind people, had set up with a team from the BBC radio program for the blind called "In Touch." Chen hoped to set up a similar radio program in China. The BBC team was delayed by traffic, so to while away the time, the delegation of blind people began playing a parlour game that involved complicated moving around in a circle and lots of giggling. Chen tried to explain the rules to me, but he was chuckling too much for me to make any sense of what he was saying. Then the BBC people arrived, and to my regret, I am now writing about Chen Guangcheng without ever really having spoken to him about his work. All I have is an image of a handsome, self-confident man in dark glasses laughing as he tried to explain a game I didn't understand.

A couple of days after our brief meeting, Chen was kidnapped in Beijing and taken back to his home in Linyi, which was then surrounded for more than a year by as many as two hundred police and hired goons. He was prevented from leaving, and anyone wanting to visit him was prevented from entering. During that year, his neighbours intervened on a number of occasions, when the men surrounding Chen's home attacked people who tried to visit, and beat Chen and his wife when they protested. Finally, Chen was accused of provoking these incidents, charged with "gathering a crowd to disrupt traffic" and "inciting the destruction of public property." He was sentenced to four years and three months in prison.

"Even if this idealistic and peaceful blind man had been genuinely guilty of the charges, the sentence is wildly disproportionate to the alleged offences," says Cohen. "This not only confirms the lawlessness and vindictiveness of the authorities of Linyi City. It is another shameful demonstration that all those in China who take seriously the regime's policies and legislation trumpeting 'a socialist rule of law' do so at their peril."

There is absolutely no doubt that the details of Chen's case, and the flagrant injustice of his punishment, are known to Chinese leaders, up to and including those at the very top. A deliberate decision was made to let the thugs in Linyi City punish someone who had the guts to stand up to them. The security apparatus believes the fear of arbitrary arrest and detention is an important deterrent, a tool for maintaining stability. Chen free, and winning cases, is a shining — and dangerous — example for others to follow.

Even so, it is possible to see the beginnings of a transference of fear. In the early 1990s, the Fan sisters were afraid of naming names and reluctant to criticize the Communist Party beyond complaining about "*them*." Ten years later, more and more people were willing to challenge authority. Now it is the party itself that is beginning to fear citizen activism. They locked up Chen because they are afraid of him and his kind.

Consider the following statement, which might seem at first glance to be a dissident manifesto:

We need to ensure people's rights to democratic election, democratic decision-making, democratic management, and democratic oversight. It means we need to create conditions for people to oversee and criticize the government. It means we need to ensure that everyone enjoys all-round development in an equal, fair, and free environment and that people's creativity and independent thinking are fully released. It also means that we need to run the country according to law, improve the legal system, and strengthen the rule of law.

These words were said by Premier Wen Jiabao in March 2007.

"China is caught in the middle," explains Jerome Cohen. "Is it going to go ahead and insert a Western-style legal system into Chinese political culture, or is it not? The question is, will the government continue to resist real legal change? Does the government want real judicial independence? I don't think it does. You would have to have a profound change in leadership."

And yet, both the leaders and their most trenchant critics both *say* they want exactly the same things. China had its People Power revolution in 1949, and there seems to be no desire, on either side, for another one.

"I hope change will be gradual," says Wu Qing, who is more optimistic than Jerome Cohen. "People at the top are changing, party officials and government officials are getting younger, they're better educated, and they have been exposed to the Western part of the world. They want to learn."

In the Philippines and Indonesia, people took to the streets to overthrow dictators. In Eastern Europe, People Power overthrew a system imposed from outside. For a time, I thought there were strong parallels between these events and the street demonstrations in China in 1989, but I was wrong. The real parallel is between the revolutions outside of China in the 1980s and 1990s, and what happened in China in 1949. Chinese who want to see changes in China today are not looking for another revolution. They are looking for an honest follow-up to the first one.

"What was the happiest time of your life?" I once asked the old Long Marcher, Zhang Qingyi. "Heavens . . . The happiest time . . . ?" He paused for thought, then gave an answer that could have been the vapid and well-rehearsed equivalent of a beauty queen's desire for world peace. But I have no doubt it was an utterly sincere response. His face changed, and he threw his shoulders back with a broad grin, becoming again a twenty-eight-year-old soldier learning that his war was won in 1949. "My happiest moment was hearing our Mao Zedong declare the foundation of the People's Republic of China from the Tiananmen Gate. We heard it on the radio. I remember listening to all the details of who would be on the state council, and who the members of the politburo would be. I was completely happy."

Zhang Qingyi's disappointment, and that of so many others, is that a righteous revolution fiercely fought and fairly won has not been followed up with more justice, and equally important, more truth.

· 4 ·

DENIAL

"We can easily forgive a child who is afraid of the dark; the real tragedy of life is when men are afraid of the light."

— PLATO

I rather miss the Berlin Wall.

Travelling from West Berlin to East Berlin was a time-consuming nuisance, but the transition from the bright lights and bustle of the West to the glum repression of the East was an amazingly surreal experience. Foreigners and members of the Allied forces crossed at Checkpoint Charlie. The process required the traveller to submit to a series of searches and interrogations while navigating a maze of rooms and corridors presided over by stone-faced border guards. The passport officers sat on a platform behind a raised counter and looked down at those seeking to pass through. A mirror placed at a forty-five-degree angle at the top edge of the wall behind the supplicant gave the guards a clear view of the entire room, so they could spot anyone trying to creep past on the floor.

Crossing by train also involved an interminable wait at the border while officials inspected every passenger's papers and searched the train inside and out. Even when all my papers were in order, and I had no contraband of any kind, I always felt that I was about to be found out, that I must be guilty of something.

Once when I was travelling from Warsaw to Berlin, I was carrying cassettes that I knew the East German border guards might confiscate. As the hours passed, I chatted with the British teacher in the seat opposite, while consuming my stock of beer and Scotch as we rattled toward the border.

"Do you always drink like this?" she asked.

"I'm worried about the frontier," I said.

I can remember nothing else of our casual conversation, and nothing much about her, but the question, and my evasive answer, have stuck firmly in my mind ever since. I had brushed off years of concern and criticism from family, colleagues, friends, and police, but the puzzled curiosity of a complete stranger made an indelible impression. It happened more than once. A hockey player in a bar in Rouyn-Noranda, Quebec, in 1977, a doctor in Montreal in 1972, and a Peace Corps volunteer on a development project in West Africa in 1965 all said the same thing: "Do you always drink like this?" During my twenty-five years of drinking, I refused to listen to anyone close to me, but somehow I could hear disinterested strangers telling me something was wrong, even though I was not yet ready to pay attention.

In the world of alcoholism treatment, denial is more than simply saying something isn't so. It is a technical term for the state of mind that minimizes, evades, and refuses to acknowledge the true nature of the addiction and its consequences. Denial is what kept me drinking long after it stopped being fun.

Facing the truth is a moral issue, but also a practical one. Maintaining lies has debilitating and destructive consequences for societies as much as for individuals. The communist system lasted as long as it did in Eastern Europe largely because its leaders refused to acknowledge the bankruptcy of their beliefs. Communism was finally overthrown in country after country in 1989, but recovery from those dark years of poverty and repression has been hampered by a failure to acknowledge the truth. The habit of denial is hard to break.

When I crossed through Checkpoint Charlie from West to East Berlin on the morning of November 9, 1989, a strange thing happened. The guard searching my luggage pulled out my Sony Walkman, a common enough toy in the West at the time, but a novelty to an East German.

"*Was ist das?*" the guard asked.

I switched it on and offered him the headphones. The Rolling Stones song "Let It Bleed" was playing at full volume in full stereo. At first, his face registered utter shock. Then he boogied behind his table for a few seconds, before handing the headphones back to me with a broad smile, the first I had ever seen on an East German border guard's face.

I spent the rest of the day waiting for the results of a crisis meeting of the Communist Party Central Committee. Just a few weeks earlier, on October 18, 1989, Erich Honecker, the leader of the German Democratic Republic, had resigned after eighteen years in power. His successor, Egon Krenz, had given East Germans the right to thirty days of travel a year and opened the route through Czechoslovakia, hoping this would slow the exodus from East Germany. The country had been hemorrhaging citizens throughout the fall. And about two hundred thousand people had left over the past year, crossing through Hungary, Czechoslovakia, and Poland, and on to West Germany. East Germany's neighbours were having trouble dealing with the influx of people.

Dissidents and political activists had been organizing regular demonstrations for weeks. A pro-democracy group called New Forum was organizing protests. On the previous weekend, half a million or more people had marched through East Berlin shouting, "We are the People!" Hundreds of thousands more marched in other towns and cities. Their list of demands included free elections, legalization of opposition groups, freedom of speech and assembly, unrestricted foreign travel, and an end to official privileges. Puppet political parties that were founded as window dressing were cutting their ties with the government and beginning to act independently of the Communist Party. The Protestant Church, after years of servile obedience to the state, began living up to its name.

The Central Committee meeting came to an end with a press conference. The politburo member who came out to tell us what had happened was Günter Schabowski, who just a few days earlier had acknowledged that the regime was no longer trusted by anyone, saying, "We will have to get used to people thinking everything we do is a trap." Buried in all the usual gibberish of official communist discourse at his press conference, Schabowski made an astonishing announcement. "Today the decision was taken that makes it possible for all citizens to leave the country through East German border crossing points," he said.

"Does that mean they can use the crossing points at the Berlin Wall?"

"Yes."

He stalked out without elaborating.

I could not believe what I had just heard. I was sitting at my typewriter trying to figure out what it all meant when a friend phoned from Checkpoint Charlie.

"The Wall is open," he said. "You have to get down here, it's going crazy."

Reporting is never as satisfying as when something momentous and completely unexpected happens. No one has time to consider what position to take, or to think about what they ought to say. What people do and say is completely spontaneous.

By the time I got to the Wall, tens of thousands of East

Germans were swarming through the crossing. West Germans spilled out of their homes and rushed down to the Wall to greet them. A remarkable number turned up with sledgehammers, determined to make a symbolic start on demolishing 156 kilometres of concrete. The entire city turned out for the biggest party Berlin had ever seen. People waved bottles, blew trumpets, cheered, sang, and linked arms with total strangers to dance on the wall that had divided the city since 1961.

The next morning, more hordes of East Germans chugged into West Berlin in their battered little Trabant cars affectionately known as "Trabis," on farm tractors, and on trucks to gawp at the big city. They wandered around the opulent department and grocery stores, and joined long lineups that stretched for several blocks outside branches of the Beate Uhse sex-shop chain, for a glimpse of the capitalist decadence they had all been warned about for so long.

November 9 was a Thursday. Nobody went to work the next day, and East Germans poured into West Berlin throughout the weekend. There was some anxiety that people, fearing the East German regime would reverse its decision, would try to stay permanently. But on Sunday afternoon, I went to the Potsdamer Strasse crossing to see them streaming back to East Berlin. Many had grim expressions on their faces. I stopped to talk to one man who was carrying a big chunk of the Wall as a souvenir. He would have been shot for approaching it just a few days previously.

"We have to get the government out," he said. "They're pigs. They've put us down for forty years. Enough is enough. We have to get rid of them, and we have to do it ourselves."

The party bosses were still hoping that promises of reform would persuade people to let them cling to power, but it was not to be. The people had had enough.

Of all the states transformed by the collapse of communism in 1989, East Germany was the only one to disappear completely.

There was simply no reason for its existence once the Soviet Union lost the will to fight for its empire and the local Communist Party lost the will to defend a failed system. Many East Germans did think there was something worth preserving in the world's most efficient police state, and West Germans worried about the cost of reunification, but once the Wall was breached, the process was unstoppable. The two Germanys became one within the year.

A week after the fall of the Berlin Wall, another revolution was brewing. In Czechoslovakia, students had been cornered and beaten up by riot police as they marched to mark the fiftieth anniversary of the death of Jan Opletal, a student who had been murdered during the Nazi occupation. They began a strike, and actors and theatre employees joined them. Theatrical performances were replaced by protests, and posters denouncing the regime were posted around the country.

I wanted to go directly to Prague, but Romania, a country that seemed to be unaffected by the winds of change, was granting visas to foreign journalists to attend the Fourteenth Congress of its Communist Party. Such opportunities were rarely offered. I took a break from revolutions and went to Bucharest.

One of the first things I noticed was a pyramid of eggs in the window of a shop opposite the hotel housing international journalists on Nicolae Ceaușescu Boulevard. There were never any customers because the eggs weren't there for Romanians to buy. They were on display for reporters to notice. The implication was that food was as abundant as the people's love for Nicolae Ceaușescu, otherwise known as "The Conductor," "Alexander of the Carpathians," "Brilliant Genius of the Romanian Nation," and "Genuine Thesaurus of Luminous Social and Political Thought."

Ceaușescu's six-hour speech to the three thousand delegates at the Fourteenth Party Congress was interrupted by frequent standing ovations. He shared the podium with his wife, Comrade

Academician Doctor Engineer Elena Ceauşescu. They were the Juan and Eva Perón of Eastern Europe. In the 1960s and 1970s, Ceauşescu's regime had been regarded as an ally by the West because the government, like Yugoslavia under Tito, often pursued policies independent of the Soviet line. But by 1989, Ceauşescu had led his country into a dead end of poverty and squalor, and his cult of personality was propped up by a secret police force called the Securitate, that was more vicious even than East Germany's Stasi and Czechoslovakia's StB.

The psychopathology of Ceauşescu's dictatorship included an almost erotic fascination with cement, so food production took second place to the transformation of villages into concrete agro-industrial complexes and the construction of palaces and boulevards. At the same time, the Brilliant Genius of the Romanian Nation enforced a rigorous program of austerity in an attempt to pay off the entire national debt of more than twenty billion dollars in less than ten years.

Bucharest was illuminated by what appeared to be a handful of forty-watt bulbs. There was no sign of any organized opposition, and the very few brave voices that dared to criticize the government were quickly silenced. It seemed as though Ceauşescu and his thugs would rule indefinitely.

After the Romanian Party Congress, I quickly returned to Berlin, where the repercussions of the fall of the Berlin Wall were transforming Germany. But I did not stay long. The Velvet Revolution was gathering strength in Czechoslovakia. The opposition movement, the Civic Forum, had called for a general strike. It seemed as though the endgame was about to begin.

Flights out of Berlin were difficult to secure, so I called Hertz to book a modest rental car, but the only vehicle they had available was a shiny gold Mercedes. I drove down to Prague in high style, arriving in good time for the finale of the revolution. The large number of writers, actors, and musicians milling around the Magic Lantern Theatre, the headquarters of the newly formed Civic Forum, lightened the atmosphere. But many of the people involved had vivid memories of the Soviet invasion of 1968, and there was no guarantee that violence had been ruled out, either in the Kremlin or in Prague Castle.

The general strike brought the country to a standstill on November 27, but only for a couple of hours. It was held during lunchtime, so as not to cause too much economic disruption. About three-quarters of the population took part. I asked some citizens why the strike had been so short. Surely, I suggested, an indefinite strike would topple the regime faster.

"We are trying to slow things down. A chaotic collapse would make it difficult for an orderly transition, and who knows what could happen?" I was told.

The turning point came two days later, on November 29, when the clause guaranteeing a leading role for the Communist Party was removed from the constitution. Without a monopoly on power the party was effectively finished, but it clung to nominal power for a few more weeks.

By early December, snow dusted the crowns of the stone saints lining the Charles Bridge, and most Czechs were still waiting patiently for the inevitable final collapse of the party. Only students continued to demonstrate in the streets. On December 10, they turned out as they did every year for a joint commemoration of the anniversary of John Lennon's death and International Human Rights Day. The Beatles' *White Album* had been released almost twenty years earlier, in November 1968, three months after the Soviet invasion of Czechoslovakia. For many young Czechs the songs "Revolution 1," and "Revolution 9" had provided the soundtrack for resistance to the Soviet crackdown known as "normalization." When Lennon was murdered in New York City on

December 8, 1980, a shrine was installed on the back wall of the Priory of the Knights of Malta, in a small square opposite the French Embassy in Prague.

People were crammed into the square singing Lennon's song "Imagine" when a young woman rushed up to the microphone to call for a change of venue. Trucks had been spotted loading documents and files at the secret police headquarters. Everyone should head over there to stop the trucks from leaving, she said. It was close to midnight by the time we got there. The students surrounded the building, but we couldn't see any trucks. Eventually, a man wearing a sheepskin coat came out to talk with the students. He was affable and calmed them down with his air of quiet authority. "I understand your point," he said, "but you're in the wrong place. This building belongs to the espionage service. We're real spies working on foreign intelligence, and we're not moving any files."

We were in the wrong place, but the rumour was true. Many secret-police files were burned that night, complicating later efforts to find out the truth about the communist years. That same day, President Gustav Husak had announced the formation of a cabinet whose majority was made up of non-communist ministers. Jiri Dienstbier, a former journalist, broadcaster, and political prisoner, was appointed foreign minister. Before the end of the press conference at the Magic Lantern Theatre, he excused himself with a smile because he was late for work. Before taking over at the foreign ministry, he had to do one last night shift stoking the boilers at an office building, the only work he could find after being expelled from the journalists' union in 1968.

A few days after Dienstbier's last night shift, news broke of a challenge to Romania's seemingly impervious regime. On December 16, the police came to evict László Tőkés, a Protestant pastor, from his house in Timisoara, the main town in the region where Romania's large minority of ethnic Hungarians live. Tőkés had been fired by his bishop, on government orders, because he had spoken to foreign newspaper reporters during the party congress and criticized the regime. The police arrived to find a crowd of parishioners determined to protect Tőkés, and prevent him from being thrown out of the house he was no longer entitled to, now that he had been dismissed. The confrontation soon turned into a bloody riot, and the army was sent in with armoured vehicles and helicopters.

I flew to Hungary immediately, hoping either to get a visa or, at the very least, to get close enough to the Romanian border to collect eyewitness reports. I had to settle for the latter. The accounts I obtained of pitched battles were entirely credible. One couple I talked to played me a recording they had made of the din of helicopters and heavy machine guns on their cassette recorder. The casualty figures they gave me, as often happens, were very much exaggerated, but there was no doubt that a serious insurrection was in progress.

I had just come back from the border crossing one day when Hungarian television news began broadcasting live a speech Ceauşescu was delivering from the balcony of the Central Committee Building in Bucharest. A crowd had been assembled in the square below. As the conductor spoke, he was suddenly interrupted by booing, hissing, and shouting. A man who had not been interrupted for years, let alone heckled, looked puzzled, and then, as if dealing with a poor telephone connection, he said, "Hello? Hello? Hello?" Shots or explosions could be heard as he was hustled off the balcony and back into the building, and the broadcast was cut.

Soon the wire services in Bucharest were reporting outbreaks of street fighting. We loaded our equipment into our van, and, with a team from an American television network who had a portable satellite dish, headed back to the border. There would be enough confusion, we hoped, that the Romanian border guards would let us pass through without visas. We got through just before the frontier was sealed and headed down Highway E-64 toward Bucharest.

We had driven to Arad, about one hundred kilometres beyond the border, when we were blocked by fighting. As we drove down the main street, we passed an armoured personnel carrier (APC) shooting at a building with its machine gun. There was return fire, and crowds of people, some armed with Kalashnikov AK-47s, were moving around the streets. We pulled into a hotel, where a group of armed, drunk, and excited young men told us we could not leave.

We stayed inside for several hours, listening to the battle, while the American technicians installed the satellite dish. We heard that units of the army had joined the revolt and were fighting against soldiers loyal to the regime and members of the Securitate. I foolishly persuaded one of the less drunk young men to take us to another hotel that supposedly was at the centre of the fighting. Tanks had surrounded the building, we were told, and Securitate men were barricaded inside.

We turned a corner to find ourselves on one side of the hotel parking lot. Three tanks stationed on the other side immediately opened fire on us. We hit the ground. From my prone position, I could see the tracers over my head, and hear the bullets chopping into the bushes behind us. Then the shooting stopped, and we didn't move for a while. After about half an hour of silence, we scrambled up and ran for the plate-glass doors of the hotel. The tanks opened fire as we reached the steps, and we raced through the doors just as they shattered, dropping the camera, still rolling, as we reached safety. My carelessness in following a guide I couldn't communicate with properly had almost got us killed.

By dawn, the tanks had gone and the city was quiet. We were able to walk back to our hotel and use the satellite dish to transmit the story. The road to Bucharest was still blocked, so we drove about seventy-five kilometres to Timisoara, the town where the rebellion had broken out. We were taken to a cemetery there, where we were shown more than a dozen mutilated corpses of people said to have been tortured by the Securitate. Now, in retrospect, it seems certain that the bodies were those of autopsy subjects taken from the morgue, not torture victims at all. The display was part of a plan, unnecessary as it turned out, to increase revulsion against the regime and to win support for the uprising. But I was gullible as well as careless that day, and reported what I saw, without asking enough questions to avoid being taken in.

We drove on to Bucharest, talking our way through roadblocks manned by peasants wielding pitchforks, shotguns, and the occasional AK-47. We found out that the uprising was being coordinated from inside the television station. Snipers made getting around extremely dangerous. The most popular rumour was that fanatical Securitate agents, including Arabs specially trained since childhood, were hiding in a network of tunnels. In the TV station itself, there were machine-gun nests in the corridors around the studio the National Salvation Front was broadcasting from. Securitate agents were said to be hiding in the air-conditioning ducts after several TV station staff were found with their throats cut.

Out on the streets, army units in tanks and APCs were still engaged in gun battles. One firefight, around the national art gallery, lasted for days because a false wall originally installed to protect paintings from sunlight concealed a secret corridor with windows overlooking the square below, and these were used as firing positions by Securitate snipers.

By Christmas Day, the revolution was over. Nicolae and Elena Ceauşescu were dead. The former leader and his wife had fled the presidential palace by helicopter, hoping to go to a military base and to lead efforts to quash the rebellion, but by that time the army had switched sides. The helicopter landed near Targoviste, where they requisitioned a small Romanian-made Dacia car, which they drove around aimlessly until they were recognized by an engineer at a steel plant and arrested by a detachment of traffic police. After a trial lasting fifty-five minutes, they were taken out and shot.

Debate continues in Romania over whether the final weeks of 1989 should be called a revolution or a coup. Certainly, ordinary people stood up under fire. They demanded the removal of a tyrant, and he was indeed removed. But the tyrant was replaced by senior members of his regime. Much of the revolution seems to have been orchestrated by the army, and there are suspicions that diehard Securitate loyalists were not responsible for all the violence. The widespread perception that the army came to the aid of a popular uprising, against a dangerous and secretive foe, certainly made it easier for the old guard to become the new guard. Dictatorships are given to paranoid conspiracy theories, and it's easy to see why people who lived under Ceaușescu for decades would reach for new ones.

Events in Eastern Europe in 1989 illustrate, among other things, the extreme difficulty of foreign intervention. At the end of the Second World War, the Soviet Union had set about its version of nation-building, from the Baltic to the Black Sea. In 1989, governments were overthrown one after the other, not just because of the failure of their economic system, but also because the indigenous populations resented deeply the communist regimes that had been imposed by the Soviet Union, and that were sustained by Soviet military force.

Transforming countries is hard work even when the motives are entirely benign, and the system installed is a workable one. The reconstruction by outsiders of West Germany and Japan after the Second World War was remarkably successful, but it is important to recall that it was preceded by the utter defeat of both nations. And the commitment of resources by the victors was unparalleled. The belief that those two countries must never be allowed to become bellicose again gave the rest of the world the determination to spend enough, for long enough, to make it work. Germany and Japan were nation-building projects unmatched before or since, and yet even they have to be regarded to some degree as works-in-progress. As long as there are Japanese and German men and women who refuse to acknowledge their wartime past, neither country can be regarded as having achieved a complete moral recovery.

After 1989, each country in Eastern Europe had to recognize what the man trudging grimly home with a piece of the Berlin Wall had told me: "We have to do it ourselves."

East Germany had more help than the others. By the time the two Germanys were reunited, West Germany had been transformed from a defeated dictatorship into a modern democracy. The country's political, economic, and cultural prosperity had been brought about through forty-five years of sustained effort. The Allied occupation, the Marshall Plan, and membership in the European Union all played a key role in its transformation. West Germany was in a position to offer unique support for the recovery of East Germany, and the two shared a common language, history, and culture. Even with that degree of neighbourly assistance, the process was much more difficult and expensive than predicted, and getting honestly to grips with the past is still troublesome.

Romania was welcomed into the European Union in 2007, but it still remains mired in the lies of the past. Czechoslovakia had a pre-war tradition of democracy to fall back on, and in Václav Havel it had a leader who saw that the fundamental problem of communism was not that the economic system did not work. The

chain-smoking playwright and thinker was alone among the leaders of 1989 to fully understand that the overthrow of communism
was a moral issue, not merely a political or economic one. But
even in Czechoslovakia, the healthy recovery from the communist
years is hampered by the partial destruction of the StB archive,
and by the unwillingness of people to face up to what they did to
each other.

In his book, *Summer Reflections*, published in 1992, Havel had
this to say about the progress his country had made since the
Velvet Revolution:

> Society has freed itself, true, but in some ways it behaves
> worse than when it was in chains. Criminality has grown
> rapidly, and the familiar sewage that in times of historical
> reversal always wells up from the nether regions of the
> collective psyche has overflowed into the mass media,
> especially the gutter press. But there are other, more seri-
> ous and dangerous symptoms: hatred among nationalities,
> suspicion, racism, even signs of Fascism, politicking, an
> unrestrained, unheeding struggle for purely particular
> interests, unadulterated ambition, fanaticism of every
> conceivable kind, new and unprecedented varieties of rob-
> bery, the rise of different mafias, and a prevailing lack of
> tolerance, understanding, taste, moderation, and reason.
> There is a new attraction to ideologies too, as if Marxism
> had left behind it a great, disturbing void that had to be
> filled at any cost.

Though they might seem to be the words of a man about to
give up in disgust, Havel still found reasons for optimism:

If a handful of friends and I were able to bang our heads against the wall for years by speaking the truth about Communist totalitarianism while surrounded by an ocean of apathy, there is no reason why I shouldn't go on banging my head against the wall by speaking ad nauseam despite the condescending smiles, about responsibility and morality in the face of our present social marasmus.

———·—·———

DR. GAO YAOJIE came to my office one afternoon in 2004 to talk about HIV-AIDS. She wore many layers of clothes against the winter chill, and a pair of old-fashioned glasses that seemed about three sizes too big. She looked more like one of the grannies who run China's neighbourhood committees than a world-famous doctor. I strained to understand her thick Henan accent as she barked out answers laden with contempt for the health department officials whose greed and incompetence had created an epidemic. "This is worse than the Japanese occupation. Worse than the Cultural Revolution," she said. "And it was all done for profit by officials and people connected with them."

Gao Yaojie, a small-town gynecologist, sounded the alarm in 1996 when many of her patients began to show symptoms that she was shocked to recognize as HIV infection. Her patients were poor villagers with no exposure to intravenous drugs, prostitution, or other common routes of HIV transmission. She realized that they had been infected while selling their own blood. When she reported the outbreak to the provincial health department, instead of shutting down the blood-collection industry that was spreading the disease, officials tried to shut up Dr. Gao.

"There is no HIV-AIDS in Henan Province," the head of the Henan health department, Liu Quanxi, told local journalists who asked about an outbreak of "a strange illness." As head of the department, Liu Quanxi had organized the spread of for-profit blood-collection stations in Henan, and many of them were owned and run by members of his family. He also set up a private company, Wanda, to deal in blood products. The health department encouraged farmers to sell their blood, and boasted that the sale of blood plasma was providing revenue for the department.

The blood-collecting stations were filthy, and the way they were run guaranteed that enormous numbers of people would be infected. The end product was blood plasma that was sold to large pharmaceutical companies. Eight hundred cubic centimetres of blood was drawn from each donor and mixed with other donors' blood in a large centrifuge. The machine separated the blood plasma from the red and white blood cells, which then were re-injected into the donors, so that they could give blood more frequently. It is, perhaps, understandable that poor peasants in a remote inland province of China were unaware in the 1990s of the dangers of being injected with other people's blood. It is inconceivable, however, that the head of the Department of Health and other officials did not know how HIV-AIDS was transmitted, and how dangerous the re-injection of commingled blood cells was. Indeed, their whole business model was based on the notion that seventy million peasants, isolated from the normal channels of infection, represented an enormously valuable reservoir of safe blood.

Dr. Gao Yaojie took her concerns to the central government in Beijing, which eventually ordered the province to shut down the blood-collection stations. But for years, the HIV-AIDS epidemic had raged unchecked. Local journalists who asked questions lost their jobs. Journalists from the national media and foreign correspondents were arrested and expelled from the province. Medical specialists sent by the central government were kept away from the areas affected by the disease and kept busy with meetings, banquets, and bogus information.

"In China the very biggest problem is telling lies," said Dr. Gao. "Low-level officials lie to high-level officials to protect themselves, and high-level officials lie to their superiors. It's a frightening problem. The liars are promoted." Dr. Gao has won national and international awards for her work, but in Henan she is treated like a criminal, and members of her family are harassed and persecuted. "During China's five-thousand-year history, emperors understood that holding power depends on winning the hearts of the people. If you lose the people's trust, you should go," she said. "Local officials told me I made too much noise, and that because I made so much noise, everyone knows about AIDS in Henan, and that's bad for the province. History will punish them. Everything I say is true, but they tell lies, nothing but lies."

When Dr. Gao came to my office, she was accompanied by a young man in his thirties with a shaved head, rimless glasses, and an intense manner. Hu Jia had worked for the environmental protection agency, but when he read about the AIDS epidemic, he quit his job to work with Dr. Gao and others trying to understand the scale of the problem and help tackle it. By visiting village after village, and carefully documenting what he saw and heard, he had become better informed about the epidemic than anyone. As he and Dr. Gao left the office, he said to me, "I have a few pictures if you would like to see them." Thinking he meant snapshots, I politely said, "Sure, bring them over." The next day he came by with seven hour-long videocassettes that he had shot in Henan. He had captured some of the most compelling images I have ever seen of China.

Hu Jia had been spending time in a village called Shuang Miao, where one of the local farmers, Zhu Jinzhong, had taken in a couple of his neighbour's children when their parents both died of AIDS. Gradually, as more and more villagers died from the disease, other children showed up at Zhu Jinzhong's home, until he had more than fifty children in residence. He renamed his house the Sunshine Home orphanage.

Hu Jia was there on the day that local officials came to shut the orphanage down. The orphanage had become famous because of a documentary about the institution shown on the national television network, CCTV. By 2003, the central government's awareness and openness about the threat of HIV-AIDS had reached a new level. National leaders had even been shown embracing AIDS patients in a symbolic gesture to counter the stigma attached to the illness. CCTV, looking for an uplifting story to broadcast on International AIDS Day, December 1, had assigned a reporter to make a program about the Sunshine Home. But press credentials from the national television network were no protection in Henan. The reporter was arrested and kicked out of the province. She courageously went back secretly to finish her program. The documentary, *55 Children With One Father*, was somewhat saccharine and sentimental, but it did draw attention to the fact that hundreds of thousands of dying peasants were leaving orphans behind. The program inspired CCTV staff to organize a fundraising drive that collected a million yuan, almost $150,000, for the Sunshine Home.

"The Henan provincial government suddenly realized that AIDS orphans are a money-making opportunity," Hu Jia told me. "The orphans attract money. The officials decided to close down Zhu Jinzhong's orphanage and build one of their own. People who want to support the orphans, whether from China or from international organizations, can donate only to the official orphanage. It's a big money tree for them to shake."

One day, a group of officials arrived in large cars with darkened windows and a bus to take the children away.

The most striking sequences in Hu Jia's videos of the Sunshine Home are interviews with elderly people who were outraged by what had happened and felt that at their time of life it was important to speak out. As I was editing my TV report, I phoned them to see whether I should use their full names, and whether they were sure they wanted their most outspoken criticisms to appear on international television. They stood by what they had said, but asked me to use their family names only. "No point in making it easy for them to find us," said one.

Wang Laoshi, a seventy-three-year-old retired teacher from Shandong Province in northern China, had read about the orphanage in a local newspaper. He was so touched that he sold his home and moved down to Henan to help Zhu Jinzhong. "I was crying when I read about those children. It reminded me of my own bitterly hard childhood," he told Hu Jia. "I decided I had to do something to help. I get up first thing in the morning and do laundry before teaching classes," he said, removing his big tortoiseshell glasses to wipe his eyes with a large handkerchief. Sad memories slowly turned to rage as he talked about the officials in black jackets who were smoking and laughing while the children were loaded onto the bus.

"The Communist Party is good!" he said, his voice getting louder. "The Central Committee is good!" Another vigorous thumbs-up. "But . . ." he was shouting now, "these people are bad, greedy, and corrupt. I have never cursed anyone in my life, but I curse their mother's dog farts!" In a towering rage, he stabbed his finger at the camera and said, "I have always supported the party, but now things are as dark as they can be. If the Communist Party ever falls, it will be because of this bunch of crooks. They are ruining the country. They are liars, traitors, bandits, and thieves!"

"Luckily, the officials didn't really understand how small digital video cameras work. I was carrying it like this," said Hu Jia, as we looked at his tapes in my studio. He showed me how he kept the camera rolling, holding it unobtrusively down by his side, instead of holding it up and looking through the viewfinder. "Actually, the camera was pointed right at them, secretly recording. Here's where they announce the orphanage has to close."

The children had been listening attentively as one of the men in black jackets lectured them about permits and regulations, but when he told them they would have to leave, they began to cry hysterically. The camera captured one boy of about twelve, holding back tears, his bottom lip thrust forward, his fists clenched in defiance, shouting, "We won't go!" But in the end they had to pack up their few belongings, and most were taken to the new state orphanage.

Zhu Jinzhong, who had taken the children in, was a simple farmer with a calm presence and a great heart. I met him shortly after the orphanage closed. "We all began giving blood when government officials came to the village in 1993. They said it was perfectly safe, a good way to help the country and make money," he said. "I donated blood for three years. They paid forty-three yuan [about five dollars] for 800 cc. My family was in financial trouble, and we needed the money." Zhu Jinzhong was already HIV-positive himself when he began taking in the village orphans. "The government wasn't doing anything for them," he continued. "As we took in more, we were struggling to cover the cost and asked the government for help. They refused. They only began to pay attention after that CCTV fundraising drive. They took the children and they confiscated the money."

Zhu, who died from complications resulting from AIDS a few months later, had compiled some statistics by talking to everyone in his village. "One thousand, four hundred and five people donated blood," he said. "Eight hundred of them have now had an AIDS test, and four hundred tested positive. One hundred and fifty-five have died so far." The provincial cover-up means that no one knows how many people altogether were infected by the blood banks, and how much further the disease has spread because people were unaware that they were HIV-positive and unknowingly infected others. The World Health Organization

(WHO) estimates at least one hundred thousand were infected with the disease. Chinese AIDS activists like Hu Jia think it could be as many as a million.

A senior WHO official I interviewed was extremely circumspect, concealing what he knew and what he felt, for fear of offending the Chinese government and making it more difficult for the WHO to work in China. The WHO official was not untruthful, but he answered almost every question with a mealy-mouthed variation on a theme. "The central government has made great progress in changing its attitude toward AIDS," he said. "And it is doing its best to tackle the problem. There are some difficulties at the local level." When the camera was turned off, he said passionately, "I hope you get those bastards!"

The power of local officials is summed up in the phrase *qiang long bu ya di tou she*, "a mighty dragon can't crush a local snake." Sometimes the central government will make an example of a provincial official caught in some wrongdoing, but corruption is so pervasive that it is impossible to punish them all without bringing down the whole system.

In 2004, I ambushed the most powerful local snake in Henan, the provincial governor, Li Chengyu, while he was attending the annual session of the Chinese parliament, the National People's Congress. I requested an interview on the subject of "The Climate for Foreign Investment in Henan Province," and after a few innocent questions on that topic to put the governor at ease, I went on to ask: "Do you think foreign investment in Henan will be affected by the epidemic of AIDS spread by unscrupulous officials operating blood banks for profit?"

The governor blamed the victims. "Blood was sold because of economic and social underdevelopment and because people lacked common sense. Blood was sold and people were infected."

"Have any of the officials involved been punished?" I asked.

"So far, we have not found anyone who was involved. It's not easy to find out which officials at which level were involved in the blood trade," he responded.

"The head of the health department, Liu Quanxi, was involved, and he's been promoted . . ."

"Why don't you go to South Africa and make a good program about AIDS? Why are you always pointing the finger at China?" he said. The governor then terminated the interview.

At the beginning of 2007, in order to conform with standards decreed by the International Olympic Committee, China revised its regulations covering foreign journalists for the first time in almost three decades. The clauses requiring prior permission for all coverage outside Beijing, and government permission for any interview with Chinese citizens, were suspended. From January 1, 2007, foreign journalists could theoretically travel freely to any part of China to interview anyone who gave their personal permission without prior government approval. It was an important change in principle, but, of course, it did not instantly bring a glorious new dawn of freedom for international journalists in China. Local police are still the police, and they will often find reasons to prevent filming. The persecution of people known to have spoken to journalists has intensified.

I have lost count of the number of times I have been detained over the years for "illegal coverage," the number of confessions I have had to write after enduring hours of lectures in the back rooms of police stations, and the number of pictures we have in our archives of people marching up to the camera and putting their hands in front of the lens. Negotiating permission to travel to another province, and dealing with the officials, known as *waiban*, detailed to accompany us, took enormous amounts of time, effort, and creativity. We do not ask permission, for example, to cover the problem of crime in a city's centre. We ask, rather, to report on the enormous strides made by the police in promoting harmony and stability in the downtown area.

In 2005, when the world was preoccupied by the risk of an influenza pandemic started by the spread of the H5N1 bird-flu virus that had originated in China, we went out to the Bai Yang Dian wetlands, a couple of hours drive from Beijing. The wetlands are a major crossroads for migratory birds, as well as home to large numbers of duck farmers. It was a perfect place to find pictures for a story about bird flu. I did not have time to go through the process of obtaining permission, and suspected it might be denied anyway. Instead, we drove to Bai Yang Dian, rented a boat, and roamed around the wetlands, stopping at duck farms. "The current situation is really not good for people in our business," duck farmer Zhang An told us. "There's no point in pretending things are good. Bird flu is a disaster for the ducks." He also told us that his ducks had been given one set of injections against the virus, and that the vaccination team was coming back the next morning to administer a second dose.

We knew we had been lucky to film all day without some busybody turning us in, and we knew that coming back would be risky, but we wanted pictures of the birds being vaccinated. Greed overruled prudence. I had an appointment I could not cancel, but I sent the cameraman back to Zhang An's farm early next morning. He got there just as the vaccination team arrived, accompanied by a squad of police and officials from the local foreign affairs office, the *waiban*. They immediately took the cameraman to the local police station and phoned me in Beijing to demand the tapes we had shot the day before. They had been questioning people, and knew exactly where we had been and who we had spoken to. "Bird flu is an issue of national importance. Your coverage was illegal, and we cannot let your colleague go until you give us the tapes," they said.

Because I was afraid the farmers would get into trouble if the authorities had the tape, I told them local people had agreed to let us take pictures, but nobody had agreed to be interviewed. I knew that a stand on principle could tangle us up for days, and guessed that officials in Bai Yang Dian would not be familiar with modern television technology, so I quickly made copies of the tapes, excluding the interviews, and drove out to hand them over. The cameraman was released after seven hours in detention. The authorities had a copy of the tapes with no interviews to incriminate our farmer friends. We had the original.

A few days later, we phoned Zhang An, the duck farmer, to see whether he had encountered any problems. He said he had not, then told us something that explained why the officials were so keen to get their hands on the tapes. The local authorities were making money by charging the farmers for the injections, which national policy decreed should be free.

Cover-ups of corruption and dishonesty are common everywhere, but the impulse to cover up bad news of any kind is particularly strong in China. The danger inherent in this tendency had been revealed by the outbreak in 2003 of Severe Acute Respiratory Syndrome (SARS), which began in southern China and killed 774 people in almost a dozen countries before it was brought under control. The alarm was first sounded in November 2002 by Canada's Global Public Health Intelligence Network, which monitors and analyzes the Internet. The network advised the World Health Organization that there were signs of an unusual outbreak of flu in Guangdong Province. China lied to the WHO until February 2003, and lied to its own people until April, when the central government imposed draconian public health measures, which it needed to publicize. Beijing suddenly became an eerie ghost town, as millions of migrant workers were told to go home, and local people were told to stay indoors as much as possible and not to mingle in public places. By that time the disease had already paralyzed international commerce and cost untold billions of dollars in damage, not just to the economies of China and Hong Kong, but to all the countries where the infection had spread.

Jiang Yanyong, a Beijing doctor, played a large part in exposing the cover-up by revealing publicly that there were more SARS patients in his hospital alone than the official figure for the entire country. He became a national hero in China. It was extraordinary to see the health minister, Zhang Wenkang, and the mayor of Beijing, Meng Xuenong, dismissed for their part in the cover-up, and it was extraordinary to hear the Chinese government apologize to the world and promise to do better in future.

When the bird-flu scare rolled around in 2005, the health ministry did a reasonable, if reluctant, job of sharing information with the rest of the world. But the agriculture ministry was obstructive, secretive, and uncooperative. China is indeed changing, but different organizations and different parts of the country are changing in different ways and at different speeds.

There will be more cover-ups, but they are becoming increasingly difficult. The Internet, where the first clues about the SARS epidemic were revealed, is a major force for change in China. There also are more whistle-blowers and more ways for them to blow the whistle, and it is harder than it used to be to silence people like Gao Yaojie and Jiang Yanyong. Whereas every aspect of life used to be seen through the lens of Maoist political correctness, and open discussion of any flaw was seen as an attack on the party itself, now the central authorities sometimes recognize the legitimacy of some public airing of problems in areas like public health, the environment, or workplace safety.

When I asked Dr. Gao whether she was afraid of speaking her mind, she said, "They're already doing as much as they can to make my life difficult and hurt my family. I'm nearly eighty. What more can they do? While we live in this world, we should always tell the truth, and never lie."

In 2004, a year after the SARS outbreak, Jiang Yanyong spoke out again, this time about the deaths and injuries he saw as chief physician of the Number 301 Hospital of the People's Liberation Army in June 1989. Many of the Tiananmen Square casualties were taken there. In an open letter to the politburo, Dr. Jiang called for a re-examination of responsibility for the army assault. He and his wife were immediately detained. After his release forty-five days later, he was subjected to a campaign of surveillance and harassment designed to keep him quiet. The Chinese government allows some latitude to people who speak the truth about present-day problems, but none whatever to those who demand the truth about the past.

· 5 ·

INTERVENTION

> "No matter how powerful one's armies, in order to enter a country one needs the goodwill of the inhabitants."
>
> — NICCOLÒ MACHIAVELLI

On May 12, 1987, the sound of the telephone wrenched me awake in a hotel room. My mind fluttered between paralysis and panic; acute anxiety clutched my chest. I did not answer right away. First, I had to figure out where I was and what I was doing there. Then I had to undo the adhesive tape I had wrapped around the phone before passing out, a precaution I had instituted some years before to discourage me from making the impulsive ranting phone calls that were starting to bring unpleasant consequences. I reached for the bottle of Scotch beside the bed and gulped a couple of mouthfuls, hoping they would stay down. The phone book next to the bottle told me I was in Lyon, France. I was ready to pick up the phone.

"Patrick?"

"Hi. You are lucky to catch me, I was just on my way out. What can I do for you?"

It was one of my bosses in Toronto.

"We would like you to come back for a meeting."

"But I am on assignment."

"Not any more. We want to discuss your future. Get a flight back, and be in my office at nine o' clock on Tuesday. Sorry."

His tone told me everything I needed to know. In any case, I knew better than to argue in my present state. The world was made of broken glass with bright lights flashing on the glistening fragments. My hands were shaking, and my mouth was dry and cracked.

"Okay. I'll see you on Tuesday."

I had been sent to Lyon to report on the trial of former Hauptsturmfuhrer Klaus Barbie, known as the "Butcher of Lyon." As head of the Gestapo in the city during the German occupation, Barbie had personally taken part in the torture and killing of prisoners, as well as ordering the transportation of Jews to death camps. He had been deported back to France from Bolivia four years earlier, and was finally about to be put on trial. The court proceedings also had the effect of confronting French amnesia about their collaboration and complicity with the German occupiers in the deportation of Jews.

Now I was confronted with my own amnesia.

I remembered leaving the pack of journalists on the courthouse steps to look for lunch. I remembered finding strawberry tarts at a bakery a few blocks from the court, buying beer at a grocery store next door, and popping the cap off the first one as I left the store. I could not remember anything after that. To this day, all I know is what I didn't do. I did not file a report on the trial of the Butcher of Lyon.

Anyone who has ever had a few drinks too many knows what it is like to have only a vague recollection of their behaviour on the previous night: the feeling of embarrassment or amusement crystallizes as the hangover clears, and gradually you remember what you said and who you said it to, what you did and who you did it with.

Alcoholic blackouts are not like that. There's no embarrassment or amusement. There is nothing at all, just a black hole where memory ought to be. My blackouts by this time bore little relation to how much I drank, or how long I had been drinking. They would begin without warning and end, sometimes days later, just as capriciously. Often I would come to in a strange hotel room, as I did in Lyon, but sometimes I would snap out of a blackout to find myself in the middle of a conversation with a complete stranger, or sitting on an airplane.

I flew back to Canada, imagining scenarios and working out strategies to save my job. I walked into the conference room at the appointed time, intending to offer rationalizations and excuses, to plead exceptional circumstances, and if none of this worked, to defy them to do their worst. But as I sat down, I was struck by a moment of complete clarity. In that moment, I realized what a nonsensical and childish waste of energy it would be to deny the truth.

"Let me save everyone some time," I said. "I admit I have a problem. I will do whatever you say." A few weeks later, I checked into a clinic in London for six weeks of treatment for alcoholism.

Over the years I have never lost my gratitude for the intervention that saved my life. Similarly well-meaning interventions on an international scale are also usually greeted with gratitude in the beginning, but as time wears on the enthusiasm for foreign help tends to wear off. Things often turn sour.

"WE HAVE NOT WITNESSED any harmful effects such as prostitution, as we did in Cambodia, and I'm proud of that."

Sergio Vieira de Mello, the United Nations top fixer of broken countries, was telling me how pleased he was with the UN's preparations for East Timor's first presidential election in 2001. As the head of the United Nations Transitional Authority, he was, in effect, the last colonial governor of a territory that was considered the last loose end of the UN's decolonization process.

I was talking with de Mello in August, a couple of weeks before 9/11. "Regime change" and "nation-building" had not yet entered the international vocabulary as euphemistic shorthand for invasion and occupation. United Nations officials had been running East Timor, half an island with a population about the size of Winnipeg, after prying it loose from Indonesia's bloody grip a couple of years before. Dili, East Timor's capital, had been burned to the ground and emptied of people in the reign of terror that followed the UN-sponsored referendum in 1999. Australia dispatched troops to restore order and supervise Indonesia's departure.

Most of the city was still in ruins. The majority of the Timorese population was still camped out among the rubble and charred shells of burned-out buildings, but the air conditioners purred softly in de Mello's office in the refurbished UN compound. In the surrounding neighourhood, reconstruction had been swift. UN staffers, civilian contractors, and aid workers spent their generous living allowances in a well-stocked supermarket, and sipped margaritas and iced lattes in the fern bars and sidewalk cafés that had sprung up to serve their needs.

It is a measure of the arrogance and immorality of many UN missions that de Mello would highlight as a proud achievement the fact that, for once, the horde of international civil servants, soldiers, and policemen arriving to help the poverty-stricken victims of unspeakable violence had not brought with them an epidemic of prostitution and sex-trafficking.

"Things could have gone wrong but they did not," de Mello continued. "If the only harmful effect is a few restaurants, supermarkets, and hotels, we should not be too concerned."

His silver-grey hair, immaculately coiffed to give just the slightest hint of ruffled boyishness, framed a handsome face. De Mello spoke four languages with suave fluency, and looked like a polo player in an advertisement for watches that cost more than my car. I knew several female journalists and aid workers who had accepted his invitations to dinner, and others who had declined. Both groups called him "Serge the Urge," and I sensed lingering affection among those who had been dinner guests, a tinge of regret among those who had not. He was a very attractive and accomplished man, and I cannot say I did not admire and even envy him a little.

De Mello was one the best and brightest of the many gifted and dedicated people who serve at the world body. A long career in central Africa, the Balkans, and Cambodia had made him the UN's number-one nation-builder, a career that requires a deep streak of optimism to overcome the frustration and disappointment that are the hallmarks of almost every attempt at intervention.

He compared East Timor with Cambodia because we had met there in 1992, during an offensive orgy of UN extravagance, waste, and self-indulgence. The collective achievement of thousands of UN employees, police, and peacekeeping troops, working in lavish comfort with large but poorly audited budgets, was the legitimization and consolidation of a thuggish regime, and the introduction to Cambodia of new strains of venereal disease, including HIV-AIDS.

The story of twentieth-century Cambodia reads like one of the Marquis de Sade's tales of repeated debauchery and rescue, in which the heroine's apparent saviours always turn out to be worse than the villains they replace.

Cambodia was colonized by the French in 1863, occupied by the Japanese during the Second World War, recolonized by the French in 1945, and finally granted independence under the eccentric royal playboy, Norodom Sihanouk, in 1953. Sihanouk was deposed in a coup by the corrupt premier and former general, Lon Nol, in 1970. The coup was supported by the United States, which wanted Lon Nol's request for military aid in order to justify the extension of the Vietnam War into Cambodia. In 1975, Lon Nol was replaced by the worst villain of all, the Khmer Rouge, communist insurgents allied with the Vietcong in neighbouring Vietnam. Led by intellectuals who had developed their own apocalyptic version of Marxism while studying in Paris, the Khmer Rouge marched into Phnom Penh on April 17. Two weeks later, the South Vietnamese capital, Saigon, fell to communist forces, ending the United States's disastrous intervention.

In Vietnam, after the last American helicopter took off from the United States embassy in Saigon, the killing largely stopped. That was not the case in Cambodia. The best estimate of the number of deaths from murder, starvation, and disease during less than four years of Khmer Rouge rule is slightly under two million, about a quarter of the population.

In one of those twists of history for which the word "ironic" seems quite inadequate, it was Vietnam that decided to impose regime change after four years of brutal dictatorship, invading Cambodia in April 1979 to topple the murderous Khmer Rouge government, and capture most of the country.

It was during the long Vietnamese occupation that I joined Cambodia's catastrophe-in-progress in 1988.

"THIS IS A CAUCASIAN," said Dr. Nguyen Van Ky, plucking a skull from a basket and placing it on the table in front of him. "It must be one of the Australians or an American."

We were at Choeng Ek, a stretch of countryside outside Phnom Penh that became known as "The Killing Fields" after Roland Joffé's film of that name was released in 1984. Today, the remains of thousands of people bludgeoned and stabbed to death at Choeng Ek are tidily packed away behind glass in a memorial stupa. In 1988, they were still being dug up, washed, numbered, and placed in large baskets stacked up around the pathologists' tables.

Dr. Nguyen believed the Caucasian skull belonged to one of the Western yachtsmen who were killed at Choeng Ek after being captured off the coast and tortured at Tuol Sleng, a former high school converted into a prison and torture centre in Phnom Penh. Like the Nazis, the Khmer Rouge documented many of their atrocities, and Tuol Sleng contains thousands of haunting photographs of the people murdered there, as well as the bed frames equipped with electrical wires and other primitive instruments of torture. The rules of the prison, translated into stilted English, still hang on the wall. Their childishness and repetitiousness, the sort of thing you might see on the wall of a kid's clubhouse, add to the sinister atmosphere of the place.

1. You must answer accordingly to my questions. Do not turn them away.
2. Do not try to hide the facts by making pretexts of this and that. You are strictly prohibited to contest me.
3. Do not be a fool for you are a chap who dares to thwart the revolution.
4. You must immediately answer my questions without wasting time to reflect.
5. Do not tell me either about your immoralities or the revolution.
6. While getting lashes or electrification you must not cry at all.
7. Do nothing. Sit still and wait for my orders. If there is no order, keep quiet. When I ask you to do nothing, you must do it right away without protesting.

8. Do not make pretexts about Kampuchea Krom in order to hide your jaw of traitor.
9. If you do not follow all the above rules, you shall get many lashes of electric wire.
10. If you disobey any point of my regulations, you shall get either ten lashes or five shocks of electric discharge.

"Kampuchea Krom" in Rule 8 refers to the area on the other side of the Vietnamese border, which, in ancient times, was part of the Khmer Empire. The reference was a reflection of the Khmer Rouge obsession with the potential threat from Vietnam, and from ethnic Cambodians who live there, an obsession that became a self-fulfilling prophesy.

Immediately after taking power, the French-educated leaders of the Khmer Rouge set about remaking the country and turning Cambodians into "new people," by emptying the capital and putting people to work on collective agricultural and dam-building projects. The early failures of this bizarre form of fundamentalist communism were blamed on intellectuals and spies for Cambodia's neighbour and historical enemy, Vietnam. An increasingly isolated and suspicious regime began the systematic liquidation of opponents, real or imagined.

As their paranoia gathered intensity, the Khmer Rouge leaders began purges of their own ranks. Many cadres, who could see that they might soon end up in Tuol Sleng or one of the many other torture and execution centres, fled to Vietnam. Among them was a young Khmer Rouge commander from eastern Cambodia named Hun Sen, who crossed the border to join the nucleus of a Cambodian exile army in Vietnam.

When Khmer Rouge leaders began launching attacks across the border to punish the defectors, they played into the hands of their much stronger neighbour. The Vietnamese army invaded Cambodia in January 1979, capturing most of the country, and pushing the Khmer Rouge back into jungle strongholds in northwestern Cambodia along the Thai border. The Vietnamese installed a puppet regime that included Hun Sen, who was still in his twenties, as foreign minister. He rose through the ranks to become prime minister by the time I arrived in Phnom Penh, nine years into the Vietnamese occupation.

After spending a morning among the piles of skulls out at Choeng Ek, and an afternoon in the torture chambers at Tuol Sleng, I was taken to interview the prime minister in the early evening. He padded into the room wearing sandals, a shirt, and cotton trousers. He was soft-spoken, unassuming, and seemed genuinely interested when I told him what the pathologist had said to me.

"Whether the remains turn out to be American or Australian," I said, "I am sure that Western countries would see an invitation to send experts to examine them, and perhaps take them home, as a very positive gesture."

"We are doing everything we can to persuade the international community to stop supporting the Khmer Rouge Pol Pot clique and recognize this government," he said.

Like almost everyone else, I like to think I am a good judge of character, but in this case, history would prove me ridiculously naive and just plain wrong. I read Hun Sen as a simple, honest resistance fighter turned politician who was devoted to doing the best for his country. He turned out to be a greedy thug. Still, on the issue at hand — recognition and assistance for a government that was trying to rebuild a shattered country — he had a point.

Nine years had passed since the defeat of the Khmer Rouge. It was known beyond doubt that they had committed one of the grimmest genocides of a genocidal century, and yet a Khmer Rouge representative still sat in Cambodia's seat at the United Nations in New York, and continued to sit there until 1993. It was as if Nazi war criminals hiding in the jungles of South America had continued to control Germany's seat at the United Nations for fourteen years after the defeat of the Third Reich.

The United States, resentful of its humiliation in Vietnam, and China, which had its own quarrel with the Vietnamese, dragooned the rest of the world into refusing to recognize Hun Sen's government on the ground that it had been installed by an illegal invasion. Worse, the United States, China, and their various allies continued to give military and financial support to the Khmer Rouge and to other guerrilla groups fighting against the Vietnamese occupation.

Full understanding of the true motives for Vietnam's project of regime-change and nation-building in Cambodia will have to wait for Vietnam itself to allow access to its archives. It is entirely possible that this was communist imperialism on a small scale, an attempt to build a greater Indochina on the Soviet model. If so, it was doomed to failure. You only have to listen to Cambodians talking about Vietnamese and Vietnamese talking about Cambodians to realize it could never work. The cultural, linguistic, and historical baggage was just too great for the Cambodians ever to accept it. The border between Cambodia and Vietnam is where Indian and Chinese influence meet. Cultural roots on one side can be traced back through the millennia to the *Bhagavad-Gita*, and on the other side to the analects of Confucius. In the French colonial notion of Indochina, Cambodia represented "Indo" and Vietnam "China." The Vietnamese stereotype the Cambodians as lazy good-for-nothings who would rather sit under a banana tree waiting for fruit to drop than do an honest day's work, while Cambodians stereotype the Vietnamese as humourless, literal-minded bullies. Whatever Vietnam had in mind when it crossed the border, the result of the invasion was the removal of an odious regime.

Before meeting Hun Sen, we had driven around the Cambodian countryside, bumping along muddy roads cratered with shell holes at about fifteen kilometres an hour, visiting hospitals without doctors, schools without teachers, and monasteries without monks. Angkor Wat, the ruins of the capital of the Khmer empire that once stretched from Burma to Vietnam, was deserted. The ethereal temples and enigmatic statues of carved sandstone seemed to float in the jungle mist, visited only by bats and cicadas, and surrounded by a guerrilla army forty-thousand strong.

Chhay Songheng, our diminutive government translator, had survived the Khmer Rouge years by concealing the fact that he spoke English. He guided us through minefields that are now tramped upon by thousands of tourists a day, and trembled every time we approached anyone carrying a gun, especially Vietnamese soldiers who had the same difficulty distinguishing between their enemies and local civilians that American GIs had had back in Vietnam.

One night after a banquet offered by local officials, the girls from the provincial dance troupe led everyone in the sinuous circles of the *rumvong*, the national dance that had been banned by the Khmer Rouge. Chhay, less than five feet tall, wove fluidly through the other dancers, a great dreamy smile on his face, as if the slow, hypnotic motion could sweep away the bitter past. Cambodia was under Vietnamese occupation, but its people were slowly coming back to life.

"The Vietnamese can't dance, and we hate them," he said, as if stating an obvious link between the two facts. "But they rescued us, and we are grateful."

Chhay's opinion seemed to be universally shared. At the newly reopened Phnom Penh University medical faculty, which by that time had two thousand students training to replace all those murdered doctors, the young men and women I spoke to all said the same thing: "The Vietnamese saved us, but it is time for them to leave." Cambodia had become Vietnam's Vietnam, and the

Vietnamese were working hard to find a way to pull out.

After interviewing Hun Sen, I flew to Thailand to join up with one of the guerrilla groups fighting the Vietnamese, the Khmer People's National Liberation Front (KPNLF). We spent two weeks behind Vietnamese lines, walking through the same jungles we had filmed from the towers of Angkor Wat a couple of weeks before.

There were three guerrilla armies contesting eastern Cambodia with the Vietnamese. The KPNLF, led by political figures from the pre–Khmer Rouge days; the royalist faction called the Sihanoukist National Army; and the Khmer Rouge. Although the three groups were considered to be bitter enemies, they were in constant radio contact with one another, and with Hun Sen's national army, so as to avoid unnecessary bloodshed. The only ones out of the loop were the Vietnamese.

The unit I travelled with was commanded by the chief of operations of the KPNLF's elite G-3 unit, Lay Bun Song. His officers had been trained by members of the British Special Air Service regiment at a secret base in Malaysia, and the troops were wearing brand-new uniforms and carrying new M-16 assault rifles, M-60 machine guns, and rocket-propelled grenade launchers, all supplied by the United States. The Khmer Rouge forces were armed by China, and the Thai military, closely allied with the United States, provided support and sometimes cross-border sanctuary for all three insurgent armies. Three members of the UN Security Council were aiding and abetting the perpetrators of genocide, even as they prepared for negotiations in Paris for Vietnam's withdrawal, and the political future of Cambodia under UN auspices thereafter.

Many of my strongest memories of Cambodia conjure up nighttime images. On Christmas Eve 1988, I spent a fearful, sleepless night hiding out in a bamboo thicket, listening to the creak and rattle of Vietnamese tanks prowling the area for our small guerrilla force. On September 26, 1989, I spent the night weaving through a vast convoy of Vietnamese tanks and trucks, driving from Phnom Penh to Saigon, to reach the satellite ground station in time to file a story reporting the withdrawal of the last Vietnamese troops from Cambodia. And on November 14, 1991, in the hours before dawn, I waited with the huge crowds of Cambodians lining the streets to catch a glimpse of Norodom Sihanouk, the one unifying figure in the tangle of modern Cambodian history, returning home to be king once again.

The departure of the Vietnamese had been the signal for the United Nations to begin deploying thousands of aid workers and showering billions of dollars on Cambodia. The vast majority of the budget was spent on the care and protection of the international community itself. Office workers had to have their own personal four-wheel-drive vehicles, and everything had to be imported. Not even vegetables were purchased locally. The average annual income in Cambodia was $140, almost exactly the same as the average *daily* allowance given to UN staffers on top of their generous salaries. Each refugee returning to Cambodia to start life anew received fifty dollars, the cost of a lobster lunch in one of the new restaurants opened in renovated French villas near the UN compound.

In November 1992, the UN ordered a consignment of half a million condoms to be shipped to Phnom Penh, after more than twelve hundred cases of sexually transmitted diseases, including HIV, were reported among UN peacekeeping troops. Before the arrival of more than twenty-thousand troops and civilians in Cambodia, HIV-AIDS was almost unknown. By the time they left, Cambodia had one of the highest rates of infection in Asia. This was partly because so many soldiers from high-risk areas brought the virus with them, but also because of the extreme promiscuity of peacekeepers who consorted with the poor and ill-educated population. For example, a United Nations Joint Programme on

HIV-AIDS (UNAIDS) study reported that 45 percent of Dutch peace-keepers had sex with commercial sex-workers or other local people during a five-month tour of duty. The head of the mission, Yasusi Akashi, told staff at a meeting discussing the disgraceful behaviour of international troops and police, "Boys will be boys."

In May 1993, the elections were held at last. The United Nations mission declared the vote to be free and fair, and then ignored the results in favour of a cumbersome deal that installed two prime ministers, Hun Sen and Sihanouk's son Prince Ranariddh. It was an unworkable arrangement that Hun Sen resolved by putting tanks on the streets, forcing his co–prime minister to flee the country, and establishing a thuggish kleptocracy that has raped the country's resources and further prostituted its people. Deprived of international support and weapons, the Khmer Rouge withered and died, as did its leader, Pol Pot, in 1998. With each passing year, the chances of any effective or meaningful war-crimes trial, truth-and-reconciliation commission, or lustration process become slimmer and slimmer. The skulls of Choeng Ek became a sanitized museum exhibit, and a regime run by a former Khmer Rouge commander has no interest in digging up any more of the past than it absolutely has to.

THE FIRST TIME I SAW Eurico Guterres, he was on stage playing air guitar as a Creedence Clearwater Revival song played over the loudspeaker. It was August 1999, and the people of East Timor were about to vote in the referendum on independence.

East Timor, a Portuguese colony since the 1500s, had been invaded and annexed by Indonesia when Portugal abandoned its overseas empire in 1975. Almost a quarter of a century later, the United Nations took advantage of the chaos in Indonesia, following the demise of the Suharto dictatorship, to give the East

Timorese a chance to break away. Indonesia was persuaded to agree to a referendum organized by the UN. Guterres was a leading figure in the campaign for a vote to remain part of Indonesia.

"When I was a little bitty baby . . ."

Guterres had a frizzy, trailer-trash, mullet hairstyle, shortish at the front, with an unruly beavertail at the back hanging down over his black T-shirt. He was thrashing away on his imaginary guitar and singing out of tune, while a retinue of overweight, gum-chewing biker chicks flopped about behind him.

"My mama would rock me in the cradle . . ."

Anywhere else, Guterres, at twenty-eight, would have been settling into a long career of pumping gas and petty crime. In East Timor, he was the leader of the Aitarak militia, recruited and directed by the Indonesian special forces, with instructions to kill, burn, and intimidate on behalf of the pro-Indonesian side in the referendum.

"In them old cotton fields back home."

I finally got to speak to Guterres at the funeral of one of his foot soldiers, a Jimi Hendrix look-alike called Placido Ximines. Ximenes had been killed in a street fight with pro-independence supporters, and his funeral was a big show of force for Aitarak. Hundreds of militiamen, in their black T-shirts, red berets, or red-and-white bandanas, the colours of the Indonesian flag, rumbled out to the cemetery on their motorcycles, behind the truck carrying Ximines's coffin. Guterres, who had threatened many times to kill journalists covering the referendum, stared past me as he answered my questions.

"What if people vote for independence?" I asked.

"There will be massive fighting. This place will be a sea of fire."

As a taste of what was to come, the Aitarak motorcycle horde drove from the funeral to attack the Becora district, a stronghold of the independence movement. A crowd of militiamen chased a man down a street close to the UN headquarters. He seemed to be getting away when he tripped and fell. They were on him in moments, hacking him to death with machetes, and then wiping their blades on his clothes before strolling away.

I have been a witness to this kind of grunting, medieval violence only in Indonesia. Elsewhere, I have seen bombs, guns, rockets, and grenades do their lethal work. But the weapons of choice after the collapse of this thirty-two-year dictatorship were machetes, swords, homemade pistols, and bows-and-arrows. Primitive combat at close quarters is somehow more vile than most modern military operations, because the intent to kill and the deed are so intimately connected. Watching a man being chopped into pieces has quite a different emotional impact than seeing shells kill dozens as they land across a valley.

Eurico Guterres, the other militia leaders, and the Indonesian military made no secret of their murderous intentions in the event of a Yes vote in the referendum, and yet the United Nations failed to take the threat seriously. The world body did little to protect the East Timorese from the bloodbath that it helped to bring about. After the UN first arrived to organize the referendum about, fourteen hundred people were killed, and about two hundred and fifty thousand were forcibly displaced to West Timor, the half of the island that, through the accident of having been colonized by the Dutch instead of the Portuguese, remains part of Indonesia.

By dawn on referendum day, there were long lineups outside the polling stations, as almost every single registered voter turned out to cast a ballot. "Whatever the outcome of the ballot, the eagle of liberty has spread its proud wings over East Timor," said the UN secretary-general's special envoy, Jamsheed Marker, gleefully flying around in his helicopter in a mood of bombastic self-congratulation.

Four days later, when the results were announced showing that almost 80 percent were in favour of independence, Eurico Guterres and his sponsors in the Indonesian armed forces went to work, burning, killing, raping, and looting. Smoke from dozens of fires rose over Dili as the Makota Hotel, headquarters for most of the international press corps, was surrounded by mobs of militiamen supervised by Indonesian officers. The crew operating the satellite dish on the roof began dismantling their gear after a wild-eyed militiaman, who looked a lot like the late Placido Ximines, raced through the hotel firing indiscriminately.

"We can no longer guarantee the safety of foreign journalists," said one of the Indonesian officers. A convoy was organized to the airport. Before the week was out, the United Nations mission, which had promised never to leave East Timor, decided to do just that, abandoning a compound that was surrounded and under fire.

Senior officials also planned to abandon thirteen hundred East Timorese who had managed to scramble through the wire to take sanctuary inside the UN compound. Only after a mutiny by junior staff was that decision overturned, and the refugees allowed to board evacuation flights to Darwin, Australia, along with the UN contingent.

A couple of weeks later, under intense international pressure, the weak Indonesian government under Suharto's successor, his former yes-man B. J. Habibie, agreed to allow a force of two thousand Australian troops into East Timor to restore order. We turned around to go back to Dili.

When we arrived, almost every building had been burned to the ground, but journalists found an abandoned convent school that was mysteriously untouched by looters. My team squatted in the mother superior's office, while the Indonesian army and militiamen burned most of Dili's remaining buildings and finally withdrew.

Every day we stumbled across corpses. One morning, local people took us to see a body lying beside the road that was quickly identified as the corpse of Sander Thoenes, a colleague and friend who worked for the *Financial Times*. It was later established, through eyewitness accounts, that he had been shot and mutilated by soldiers from Indonesia's Battalion 745.

Another day, we went to see the ruins of the home of a prominent independence activist, Manuel Carrascaleo. The well in the courtyard was choked with corpses. The stench was overpowering, but I couldn't move away. I peered over the parapet, mesmerized not by the ugliness of the tangle of bloated bodies, but by the beauty of the mother-of-pearl colours of decomposing skin, the delicate iridescence of coral pink and celadon green. Suddenly, the water was disturbed by splashing and ripples. My heart started pounding as I forced myself to look at what might be alive down there. I saw a turtle with a vicious-looking beak swimming around in the stew of decomposing flesh and shit that had oozed from bowels slit open before the bodies were thrown into the well.

East Timor got its independence, its flag and anthem, its president and parliament, and the first new country of the new millennium began life with the promise not only of democracy, but also of prosperity from offshore oil and gas deposits. But, by 2006, Australian troops were deployed to the territory again, as East Timor sank back into chaos, rebellion, and rioting on the eve of the country's second elections.

The number of deaths resulting from the referendum in East Timor was tiny compared with the pogroms perpetrated by the Indonesian military. Tens of thousands were killed during Indonesia's twenty-five years of occupation. Ben Kiernan, director of the Genocide Studies Program at Yale University, calculates that in proportion to their populations, East Timor and Cambodia suffered mass murder on a roughly equivalent scale, each losing between 21 and 26 percent of its population.

The United Nations, in its arrogance and haste, tidied up a

loose end of colonialism by organizing a referendum, cobbled together a new country in a mere two years, and then walked away. The UN may have learned some lessons from Cambodia, but once again, nation-building was a job half-done, and half-done badly.

Sergio Vieira de Mello, the UN official who was so proud in 2001 of not introducing prostitution to East Timor, went on to lead the United Nations mission in Iraq, after the United States and its allies embarked on a program of regime change and nation-building there. "The United Nations presence in Iraq remains vulnerable to any who would seek to target our organization," he said to the General Assembly in July 2003. Just one month later, on August 19, 2003, de Mello was killed when a truck bomb blew up the headquarters of the United Nations at the Canal Hotel in Baghdad.

WE WERE DRIVING along a road near Kompong Cham in central Cambodia in 1993 when I caught a glimpse of the Chinese flag fluttering over some large earthworks off in the distance. After driving through a gap in the high walls of banked earth, we were greeted at the camp gate, and escorted into the base to meet a polite young lieutenant named Yang, who showed us around.

The first major deployment of troops from the People's Liberation Army, wearing the blue berets of United Nations peace-keepers, had come under attack two nights before. Three Chinese soldiers had been killed by rocket-propelled grenades. They were part of a force of eight hundred engineers sent to build roads and bridges in Cambodia.

Lieutenant Yang showed me some unexploded rounds left over from the attack. They had been made in China. He declined to comment on the irony that weapons China had supplied to the Khmer Rouge were now being used to kill Chinese soldiers. "I'm a soldier. I can't comment on politics," he said. "Anyway, we're not sure whether they were deliberately fired at us, or if they were stray rounds from fighting between the Khmer Rouge and government forces."

The Chinese had become a target because they had abandoned support for the Khmer Rouge, and joined the rest of the world in a mission that the Khmer Rouge regarded as interference in the internal affairs of Cambodia. Until 1988, China was radically opposed to United Nations peacekeeping missions. Not only did it refuse to send troops abroad, but China also refused to contribute money or resources to peacekeeping operations. This stand was based on what now seems to be a fundamentalist interpretation of the cornerstones of China's foreign policy: the Five Basic Principles of Peaceful Coexistence. These principles — mutual respect for sovereignty and territorial integrity, mutual non-aggression, non-interference in each other's internal affairs, equality and mutual benefit, and peaceful co-existence — have been the mantra of Chinese diplomats since Premier Zhou Enlai first intoned them in 1953, during negotiations with India on Tibet. They are so deeply embedded in Chinese thinking on international affairs that they have been written into the constitution.

Their all-time favourite among the five is number three: non-interference in the internal affairs of others. This position is used to justify China's unwillingness to consider outside views on Taiwan and Tibet. It also justifies heavy investment in rogue states, and China's use of its Security Council veto in support of countries like Iran, Zimbabwe, Burma, North Korea, and Sudan. "Business is business," said Deputy Foreign Minister Zhou Wenzhong in 2004, when asked about China's position as the largest investor in Sudan, despite the regime's murderous conduct in Darfur. "We try to separate politics from business."

China still recites the Five Basic Principles mantra frequently, but the strict interpretation that suited isolationist China began to outgrow its usefulness when the country needed to co-operate with the rest of the world to get its economy moving in the 1980s. By joining UN peacekeeping missions, China indicated that it wanted to be seen as a benign, responsible member of the world community, even though its world view still differs significantly from that of Washington, Moscow, Paris, or London. While the basic shift in approach brought the country more closely in line with the rest of the world, China continued to consider itself the great exception.

Times have changed since 1793, when the Qianlong emperor wrote to Britain's King George III explaining his dismissal of a British mission seeking greater trade with China: "Our dynasty's majestic virtue has penetrated unto every country under heaven, and kings of all nations have offered their costly tribute by land and sea. As your ambassador can see for himself, we possess all things. I set no value on objects strange or ingenious, and have no use for your country's manufactures." The question of *whether* to engage with the outside world is no longer an issue for Chinese leaders, but *how* to engage has become a significant preoccupation.

Before I wound up my first posting in China in 1996, I finally obtained permission to film part of a news report at the Beijing Central Party School, where promising officials are groomed for higher posts. I wanted to get in with our camera, not because I needed to see the courses given to high-flying Communist Party members, as interesting as that might have been, but because Matteo Ricci's tomb is located in the the school grounds.

Matteo Ricci, an Italian Jesuit missionary and a brilliant linguist, mathematician, and scientist, died in Beijing in 1610 after living in China for twenty-seven years. He was the first Westerner to be granted permission to live in the country, and that permission was granted on the condition that he never leave.

Even after he had lived in China for many years, he was puzzled by the insecurity and suspicion he found in a country that was so obviously great and powerful.

> It remains hard for us to believe how such a huge kingdom with so many soldiers could live in continual fear of other states that are so much smaller, [Ricci wrote] so that they fear some great disaster every year and spare no pains to protect themselves from their neighbours either with troops or with deceit and feigned friendship: the Chinese place absolutely no trust in any foreign country and thus they allow no one at all to enter and reside here unless they undertake never again to return home, as is the case with us.

The Ming dynasty officials who let in the Jesuits needed and wanted their skills in mathematics, astronomy, and science, but were far from enthusiastic about the Jesuits' intention to convert the Chinese to Christianity. When the Jesuits began their mission in 1583, they wore humble Buddhist monks' habits. Few took them seriously. Chinese society was extremely hierarchical, and the Buddhist clergy of the time had little status compared with scholars and officials whose rank, prestige, and consequent wealth, were determined by a nationwide system of examinations in the Confucian classics. After several years, Ricci realized that he needed to win the respect of the rich and powerful to have any chance of converting China to Christianity. In 1595, he abandoned his pretensions of poverty and began being wearing purple silk robes. The plan now was to convert China from the top down:

> To gain greater status we do not walk along the streets on foot, but have ourselves carried in sedan chairs, on men's shoulders, as men of rank are accustomed to do. For we

have great need of this type of prestige in this region and without it we would make no progress among these gentiles, for the name of foreigners and priests is considered so vile in China that we need this and similar devices to show that we are not priests as vile as their own.

Ricci and his less-gifted Sancho Panza, Michele Ruggieri, began interpreting Catholic doctrine in terms of the Chinese classics. What resulted later was a schism between Ricci's belief that the greatest resonance was between Confucianism and Christianity, and Ruggieri's emphasis on similarities between New Testament concepts and some aspects of Daoism. Ricci came to believe that converts should be allowed to continue to practise Confucian rites venerating their ancestors, and the texts Ricci wrote attempted to reconcile Christianity with Chinese culture and philosophy.

Matteo Ricci and two other great Jesuit scientists who succeeded him, Johann Adam Schall von Bell and Ferdinand Verbiest, collectively spent more than a century sharing their encyclopedic knowledge of mathematics, astronomy, technology, architecture, and art with the Chinese elite. They corrected the imperial calendar, designed and constructed palaces, invented gadgets of all kinds, and even built cannons for the imperial armies. They were convinced that their indispensability and their access to the court would bring the number of high-level converts to a critical mass. Eventually, they aimed to convert the emperor himself, which would be a turning point for Christianity in China, much as the conversion of Emperor Constantine had led to the triumph of Christianity in Rome.

Ricci's attempt to reconcile Christ and Confucius led to bitter quarrels among the Jesuits, the Dominicans, and the Franciscans on the correct way to save Chinese souls. The Chinese Rites Controversy, as it became known, ended more than a century after

Ricci's death. Ricci's ideas were eventually rejected by the Pope, and Christian missionaries were banned from China by the emperor. The first concentrated Western effort to engage and change China had failed. The Chinese learned what they wanted to learn, and shrugged off the ideas that did not interest them.

As we filmed around Matteo Ricci's tomb, I explained to viewers that in the four hundred years between the 1580s and the 1980s, not much had changed in the motives and mindsets that governed the interaction between China and the rest of the world. In the 1580s, China was interested in Ricci's knowledge of mathematics and astronomy, and in his prisms and clocks, but not in his Christian ideas. In the 1980s, China's supreme leader, Deng Xiaoping, wanted Western technology and skills to raise China out of poverty. He was ready to let McDonald's, Motorola, General Motors, and Goldman Sachs into China, but he was not interested in ideas about human rights and democracy that might come with them.

Whenever Western leaders came to Beijing, they would witness a frenzy of contract-signing, and say that closer business ties and more trade would ultimately bring freedom and democracy to Chinese citizens. China's leaders believed that raising living standards was the only way the Communist Party could safeguard its monopoly on power. As in the 1580s, there was a mismatch of motives and mindsets between East and West, but this time there is a powerful shared interest in developing China's economy.

While the Jesuits hoped to use technology to change China from the top down, some of the technology China is eagerly embracing today may have the potential to change China from the bottom up. When I left China in 1996, my final report made no mention at all of the Internet. When I returned in 2003, the impact of widespread access to the Net was at the top of the list of stories I wanted to look into.

LI XINDE HAS NO PERMANENT HOME. He moves from city to city sleeping on couches offered by friends, family members, or strangers who have contacted him over the Internet with information they want him to follow up on. He is China's best-known guerrilla journalist. "I have no property . . . just my camera and my computer, and they were given to me by someone," he told me when I met him at a friend's home in Beijing.

A stocky, handsome man in his late forties, Li used to work for a big-city newspaper, but many of his stories were spiked because they were considered too controversial. In 2001, he discovered the power of the Internet when a story he had written about the party secretary of a village, who was terrorizing his neighbours by firing his gun, gained widespread attention through emails and chat rooms. One of his most famous stories, on the corruption of the deputy mayor of the industrial city of Jining, included pictures of the official on his knees, begging not to be exposed.

"It's hard for them to arrest me because I never write about politics and never break the law," Li told me. We were on our way to meet Fu Xiaohui, a Chinese-Canadian businessman who had been cheated out of some property.

Li spent hours poring over the documents provided by Fu Xiaohui. The documents backed up the businessman's contention that he had been cheated by former partners, in league with corrupt courts and police, who at one point arrested him and his wife and held them for days to intimidate them.

"I check everything," said Li Xinde.

Li Xinde's blogs are among the most popular in China. They are read by tens of millions of people, who then spread the information in emails, bulletin boards, and chat rooms. He is careful to avoid criticizing the Communist Party, and his blogs contain neither pornography nor "forbidden speech." Nevertheless, he maintains more than fifty blogs at a time, opening up new websites to replace those that are shut down to stop their content from spreading.

"If I have an important article, I can arrange someone to help put it out in fifty or sixty blogs simultaneously. I also have a server overseas, and I can post it in fifty, sixty, seventy, or eighty chat rooms all at once, and spread it everywhere."

Li Xinde likes to conduct his investigation, then skip town before his targets can retaliate. "The danger to me is not from the central government; the danger is from corrupt local officials who have some power. Those people go after me. The people I write about, corrupt officials, have committed crimes, but I am doing nothing wrong by exposing them."

I began to notice national Internet sensations in 2003. The first was in April. A young man named Sun Zhigang was picked up by police in Guangzhou, in southern China, where he was looking for work as a fashion designer. As a migrant worker without the necessary temporary residence permit, he was taken to a detention centre where he was beaten to death. A story from a local paper, the *Southern Metropolis Daily*, spread like a virus on the Internet. Sites commemorating Sun were shut down eventually, but the authorities also, to universal astonishment, changed the law so that police can no longer arbitrarily detain and expel migrant workers.

The second big campaign I noticed began at the other end of the country in October. In the city of Harbin near the Russian border, a woman named Su Xiuwen was driving a BMW when she was involved in a fender-bender with a tractor driven by a farmer named Dai Yiquan, who was hauling a load of green onions. An argument ensued during which Su lost her temper and slapped Dai. She then jumped into her BMW to escape the angry crowd that had gathered. As she tried to drive away, she lost control of the vehicle, killing the tractor driver's wife and injuring twelve others. The uproar began after she was given a suspended sentence, and the rumour spread that she was related to a senior official who had fixed the case. The clamour died down only after a retrial and the official press denied the rumours of family influence. Although the retrial verdict was much the same as the first, cyber-citizens found some satisfaction in having forced an investigation.

Internet ferment has become commonplace in China. Sometimes, as in the Sun Zhigang case, the *cause célèbre* begins with a story in a local newspaper or television station, which is then told in much more detail on the Internet. Often, it is the other way around. There is no such thing as a privately owned newspaper, but official media outlets do have to compete for readers and advertising revenue. They can no longer ignore reports that are circulated among tens of millions of people on the Net.

The Internet is a new challenge for the Communist Party propaganda apparatus, which is used to having absolute control over every syllable that is either printed or broadcast. The government now deploys a vast array of monitoring and filtering equipment and software to control what people can access on the Web. There are also tens of thousands of cyber-cops monitoring what is written by Chinese users, and Internet service providers are held responsible for removing any content deemed offensive. These measures can and do stop discussion of topics that are already taboo, such as Tiananmen Square, the Dalai Lama, Taiwan independence, or the banned Falun Gong sect, simply by blocking anything containing those key words. But unexpected developments, such as the BMW incident, can create Internet uproar before the censors figure out which key words to block.

The Great Firewall, the blocking technology that prevents access to specific sites and aborts searches using forbidden words, can easily be circumvented by using proxy servers or by subscribing to a Virtual Private Network (VPN) service. It is easier for the Chinese to get around the prohibitions on what they can read than on what they can write. The methods of bypassing the firewall make it impossible for the Internet police to check what computer is looking at what, but postings to websites or emails can always be traced back to a specific computer, through the Internet service provider. All Chinese isps must provide that information to police.

China has its own highly skilled computer engineers and software developers, but much of the technology used to control the Net has been sold to China by Western companies. If the Jesuits were willing to reinterpret their religion to suit conditions in China, it should come as no surprise that Western corporations are willing to adjust *their* principles in exchange for access to the Chinese market. The international Internet giant Yahoo caused great controversy when it helped the Chinese police locate and arrest people for what they had written online, although it was under no legal obligation to do so, since its servers are in Hong Kong. Google also attracted criticism for its co-operation with Chinese authorities, but its behaviour is less distasteful than Yahoo's. Google co-operates with the authorities by censoring searches, but unlike Yahoo, it has not turned its clients in to the police.

Despite the sophistication and scale of the government's effort to control citizens' access to the Internet, the kinds of incidents that can cause national outrage are so numerous and so diverse that it has become impossible for the authorities to keep up. In June 2007, a local television reporter in Shanxi Province, alerted by online discussions among parents of missing boys who claimed their children had been kidnapped, began reporting on the use of forced labour at kilns making bricks for China's construction boom. After years of ignoring the parents' complaints, police were goaded by the growing publicity into raiding hundreds of brick kilns, small coal mines, and similar enterprises that have difficulty recruiting workers because the work is hard, dirty, and dangerous. It turned out that the kiln owners had resorted to slavery. The police raids liberated hundreds of men and boys who had been used as slave labour in the kilns. The wounded, emaciated, filthy workers were dressed in rags and looked like concentration camp survivors. They had been beaten and attacked by fierce guard dogs. Some were maimed and unable to walk.

One of the kilns was owned by the son of the local party secretary. Another kiln boss had killed one of his workers with a shovel. The men and boys had been kidnapped or lured by the promise of good jobs, often by labour gang bosses who prey on migrant workers arriving from the countryside at city train stations looking for work. More raids and arrests followed. National television and newspapers featured party leaders ordering a nationwide investigation and crackdown against slavery.

The Internet Bureau of the Communist Party's Central Office of External Communication, which regulates Internet service providers, struggled to lock the stable door well after the horse was long gone, by issuing the following instruction:

> Regarding the Shanxi "illegal brick kiln" event, all websites should reinforce positive propaganda, put more emphasis on the forceful measures that the central and local governments have already taken, and close the comment function in the related news reports. The management of the interactive communication tools, such as online forums, blogs, and instant messages, should also be strengthened. Harmful information that uses this event to attack the party and the government should be deleted as soon as possible. All local external communication offices should enhance their instruction, supervision, and inspection, and concretely implement the related management measures.

The Internet is not the only new technology giving the Communist Party a headache. The cellphone is also having a revolutionary impact. Text messaging, favoured by teenagers in the West, is popular with the hundreds of millions of Chinese. Jokes, some quite salty and others with political overtones, circulate in their billions from one user to another. In 2005, activists used cellphone text messages to organize a campaign to boycott Japanese goods to protest the way wartime history was whitewashed in some Japanese textbooks. I was surprised when my cellphone alerted me to a message from the Public Security Bureau. The police wanted to shut the demonstrations down. "We ask the people to express their patriotic passion through the right channel, following the laws and maintaining order. Do not take part in illegal activities."

Just days after the brick kiln incident revealed that some members of China's underclass endure conditions reminiscent of the Shang Dynasty, which was overthrown by an army of rebellious slaves in 1080 B.C., about twenty thousand members of China's emerging middle class stepped into the twenty-first century by staging an unprecedented, not-in-my-backyard protest and winning at least a temporary victory.

The plan to construct a huge plant to manufacture paraxylene, a chemical used in polyester, on the outskirts of Xiamen had created a torrent of protest on Internet blogs and in chat rooms. When the government of the coastal city ignored fears that pollution from the plant could cause leukemia and birth defects, opponents took to their cellphones, asking people to demonstrate outside the city government offices. Twenty thousand showed up with placards and gasmasks. Many of them used cellphones to make videos of the event, which were then posted on the Net. The local government backed down and the national environmental protection agency announced it would carry out an investigation before permitting construction.

Cellphone technology can serve the enemies of free information, as well as its friends. I buy prepaid SIM cards to make calls when I think my usual number is likely to be tapped. Tapping is usually triggered when I begin reporting on a situation the authorities would rather keep quiet, or come into contact with people the security apparatus already has its eye on — or its ear. When I travel to cover sensitive stories, I always take the battery out of my cellphone, so that local police cannot use it to track my whereabouts. I learned this from what happened to Zhao Yan.

Zhao Yan, a former policeman and crusading journalist for a Chinese paper, was working for the *New York Times* as a researcher in September 2004, when the newspaper published a story about former president Jiang Zemin's retirement from his last post, the chairmanship of the Military Commission. It seemed to me a rather minor scoop, but the government thought otherwise and began an investigation into the leak. Zhao Yan, who had nothing to do with the story, being a specialist on countryside problems rather than leadership issues, learned that he was suspected of being the source. He told friends he was switching off his cellphone to avoid being tracked. Ten days after the story appeared, he was having dinner at a Pizza Hut in Shanghai when he spotted a cockroach in his pizza. Instinct overtook caution, and he grabbed his cellphone, switched it on, and called a friend at a local paper to tell him to come over and write a story about the unsanitary conditions at the restaurant. Minutes later, state security agents arrived and arrested him.

Zhao Yan was initially accused of revealing state secrets, but that charge was eventually dropped and replaced by unrelated fraud charges, which he denied. He was sentenced to three years in prison, served his time, and was released in September 2007.

Economic development and technology are changing China as never before, but China is no more easily converted by outside ideas today than it was four hundred years ago. Indeed, Beijing regards pressure to conform to Western notions on human rights, democracy, and the rule of law as outside interference reminiscent of the foreign carve-up of China in the nineteenth century. Matteo Ricci observed, "I am of the opinion that the Chinese possess the ingenuous trait of preferring that which comes from without to that which they possess themselves, once they realize the superior quality of the foreign product." He was perhaps right as far as merchandise goes. After all, Zhao Yan was eating pizza and talking on a cellphone when he was arrested, and it's a safe bet that the men who arrested him took him away in an Audi or a Mercedes. By the time he died, Ricci would have understood that the ideas which would have allowed Zhao Yan to work as a journalist unmolested are not being adopted as rapidly as the technology.

· 6 ·

RECOVERY

"Man's capacity for justice makes democracy possible; but man's inclination to injustice makes democracy necessary."

— REINHOLD NIEBUHR

"Hello, dear."

My mother had deteriorated since my last visit. Although she still knew me, she could no longer remember why. She did not know my name.

She talked in generalities, hoping I would fill in the blanks for her, and not notice her lack of recall. It was spring 2005. Her mind had been crumbling for years, but her pride remained intact. She did not want to reveal that she could not remember who I was.

I had some understanding of her confusion from making telephone calls on countless hungover mornings, when I tried to piece together the events of the night before, without ever admitting I had no memory of what had happened.

"Have you been getting out much?" I asked.

"Sometimes."

"Where have you been?"

Confronted with a direct question, her mind fabricated a

plausible answer from the repertoire of things she used to do. "Oh, you know, dances and things," she said.

There is no way of knowing whether she really believed this invented life, or merely hoped that I would believe it. She had forgotten her husband and her children, forgotten the places where she used to live, forgotten her own name and her age. She could sometimes remember things about her parents, or details of what her life was like in the 1930s. Occasionally she even flirted a little, believing herself to be about twenty years old and me to be a young man she had met at one of those dances. "Why did you pick me?" she asked.

Day after day, she sat beside the window of her room in an old-age home in the English midlands, her wrinkled scalp scarcely covered by wisps of grey hair, her eyes sad and withdrawn in the crumpled tissue paper of her face. Conversation is difficult with someone who cannot remember the question she is trying to answer, or the beginning of the sentence she is struggling to complete.

In the early 1980s, when she was running a craft shop in a small town in Somerset and I lived in London, my mother and I once talked late into the night about her sister, who had been struck by a mysterious early onset of senile dementia and died a mindless death before she was sixty. My mother had had a few more drinks than usual, and, of course, I had had many more drinks than she had. "If I ever go barmy like that, I wouldn't want to live," she said. "I want you to help me out of it. Don't put me away in one of those homes."

She made me promise to end her life if what happened to her sister ever happened to her. I solemnly agreed. The next day, she absolved me from my promise. "I didn't really mean what I said last night," she said.

As she slipped gradually into dementia, my mother often said that her worst fear was of losing her mind. By the time that hap-

pened, she was long past the point where she could make the decision for herself, and I was past the drunken arrogance of my promise to make the decision for her. Fortunately, alcoholism got the
better of me, long before dementia got the better of her.

I have learned not to dwell on what might have been, good or
bad, but I am convinced that, had I still been drinking when my
mother's mind faded to black, I would have felt compelled to keep
the promise I had made so casually. Since she lived until she was a
few weeks shy of her ninetieth birthday in 2006, it is more likely
that I would have died first, of organ failure or in a stupid,
drunken accident. As it was, I was able to deal with her declining
years with dignified kindness, rather than callous indifference or
self-indulgent emotion. I visited whenever I could and made sure,
with my sister, that she was well looked after.

As the sun began to set on that spring evening, she nodded off
in her chair and then woke with a start and peered across at me.
"Who are you?" she asked suspiciously.

"I'm just visiting for a while."

She looked puzzled and tried to make sense of her confusion.
"I don't think you're the man I used to know," she said. She was
right about that.

Alcoholism crept up on me by imperceptible degrees. I had as
little awareness of its progress as my mother did of her own descent
into oblivion. The difference is that my decline was reversible,
while my mother was never coming back. As I watched her wither
away, it seemed absurd to lament that a long life was coming to
a close. I witnessed the process with equanimity, punctuated by a
stab of fear every time a trivial lapse of my own memory reminded
me that my turn was coming soon.

We both gazed out the window in silence, looking out over the
manicured trees and shrubs of the garden to the fields stretching
out toward Sherwood Forest. The English language does not have

enough words for the greens of the English summer landscape. I reach for emerald, sage, jade, celadon, lime, and chartreuse, but my vocabulary fails me long before I can find words for every shade of green I can see.

"Have you had a long journey?" she ventured.

"I arrived from Afghanistan this morning."

"That's nice, dear."

It is the contrast with where I have just come from that makes the greenness of England so luminous. By tomorrow, I will stop noticing. The striking particularity of a place soon fades into the background as it becomes the new normal. I first visited Afghanistan during a drought and was overwhelmed by how brown everything was. In the golden hour before twilight, the dullest colour of the entire palette came alive. Mountains, valleys, and villages were washed in an infinite variety of sepia, walnut, and mahogany, khaki, burnt umber, and bronze. But after a day or two, the breathtaking landscape became the unnoticed backdrop to a succession of ordinary, dusty, dangerous days.

"Do you live in that place you just said?" she asked.

"No, I live in China."

"That's nice, dear."

The most conspicuous feature of China is not a colour, like the green of England or the brown of Afghanistan, but the overwhelming number of people. I have lived here for so long now that when I return to Europe or North America, I always wonder, "Where *is* everybody?" In a Chinese city, there are people everywhere, all the time.

No matter what time I go by the bus stop across the street from my apartment, there is always one overcrowded bus pulling away while a cluster of others arrive already full. Moving through the constant press of people jostling to get somewhere else often gives me the feeling I ought to drop my own plans, join the crowd, and go wherever they are going, just in case I am missing something that will be gone forever if I don't grab the chance now.

On the surface, Afghanistan and China have little in common, but there are several important parallels. The Taliban years in Afghanistan, and the Cultural Revolution in China, both were periods of self-centred isolation from which neither country has fully recovered. The West led by the United States intervened decisively in Afghanistan after 9/11 to remove the Taliban, but it has stumbled badly in helping the country find a better way to live. Military interventions in China are a thing of the past, but foreigners find it hard to resist the belief that China needs to be changed, and that they have an important role to play in bringing that change about. Neither Afghanistan nor China takes kindly to outside interference.

In the days when my mother knew who I was, she always found it astonishing that I could live in China. If we went out for a Chinese meal, her jaw would drop when I spoke to the staff in their native tongue. China was quite simply the most foreign of all foreign countries, and the Chinese the world's most foreign people. By the time I visited in 2005, she had lost awareness of both place and time. China was exactly the same as any other country; the difference between here and there had shrunk to nothing. The loss of short-term memory condemned my mother to live permanently in the present. She asked the same questions over and over. The answers evaporated the instant she heard them.

"Where do you live?" she asked again.

"I live in China."

"That's nice, dear."

I said goodbye and left for another assignment that would take me back to Afghanistan. I knew it would be months before I could visit again, but in this case, the truth seemed pointless.

"See you tomorrow," I said.

"That's nice, dear."

"WELCOME BACK TO KABUL," said Mullah Mohammed Usman Sharyar as I walked into the foreign ministry on a bright June morning in 2001.

One benefit of Afghanistan's rapid regression to the seventh century was that, almost alone among Asian cities, Kabul had breathable air. With no pollution, the night sky was stunning. Uncountable stars of diamond brightness were scattered across a deep black carpet. In the daytime, the sunshine often had a gorgeous clarity.

"You must obey the rules for foreign journalists," said Mullah Sharyar, giving me a press card. "You must not take pictures of any living thing, including yourself."

It was a rule unique to the Taliban version of Islam, an extension of the ban on representational art as a competition with God's handiwork. Making television programs would be a challenge in a place where pictures, including the on-camera reporter stand-ups, were illegal. Looking for a loophole, I reminded him I had just handed him two pictures of myself for my credentials. "Photographs are permitted for the correct administration of the Islamic Emirate of Afghanistan, and when necessary for humanitarian reasons."

Just before arriving, I had seen a piece by a colleague from a satellite news channel that contained only pictures of buildings, vehicles, and other objects. It concluded with an ingenious stand-up, consisting of an image of his shadow against a wall, as he explained the constraints he was working under. I hoped to do better than that by getting out of town. I knew from previous visits that outside Kabul the rules could be more flexible. Many a mullah could not resist the urge to appear on television and then, having been filmed himself, would then find a way to justify pictures of other living things.

A couple of years earlier on the front line north of Kabul, we

had filmed Taliban soldiers racing around in their tanks after interviewing their commander, Khalikdad Akhand, a mullah with pen-
etrating blue eyes and an engaging smile. At the time, the Taliban
had gained control of about 90 percent of Afghanistan, and was
fighting against the Northern Alliance for control of the rest. After
answering my questions about the fighting, he asked me what I
thought of President Bill Clinton's troubles over Monica Lewinsky.
I said something noncommittal and asked what he thought. "It is
absolutely not possible to negotiate with such a person," he said.
"He should be removed from office and stoned to death."

His view was an interpretation of Islamic law on adultery
shared by fundamentalists elsewhere, but by 2001 the Taliban had
left orthodox Islam far behind, and was issuing ever more eccentric and draconian decrees. Although the basis for everything was
supposedly Islamic law, the Taliban was behaving like a fanatical
revolutionary political movement, forever seeking new heresies to
root out in the quest for perfect purity. Music, dancing, theatre,
movies, television, kite-flying, and dolls were banned early on.
Men had to wear beards and were ordered not to trim them.
Women had to be covered from head to foot and were not allowed
to work. Girls were not allowed to go to school. Women's shoes
with metal studs were banned because the clicking sound was
deemed provocative. Buses were clumsily configured to separate
male and female passengers.

Canadian diplomats rarely speak above a whisper, but Ferry de
Kerckhove, Canada's ambassador to Pakistan who also handled
Afghan affairs, felt able to step out a little. "It's a bottomless pit.
And you've got the internally displaced, you've got refugees, you've
got all the symptoms of a sick society, plus you have a regime that is
unbearable, abominable," he said.

Some Taliban decisions in the spring and early summer of 2001
seemed to be a direct reaction to the regime's increasing isolation.

Buddhist statues almost two thousand years old were blown up in Bamiyan, an act of vandalism justified by the Islamic proscription on figural representation. Non-Muslims were ordered, briefly, to wear yellow armbands as proof of their exclusion from mandatory prayers five times a day. International aid agencies were accused of spreading immorality and shut down, at a time when Afghanistan was struggling with one of the worst droughts in history, and needed international help more than ever. Two hundred thousand newly displaced people who left their land to avoid starvation were added to the millions displaced by two decades of war and natural disaster. "We welcome international aid so long as the motive is humanitarian and not political. But Islam is our religion, and the Islamic Emirate of Afghanistan puts Islamic principles first," said Mullah Sharyar.

At the time, bakeries run by the World Food Programme (WFP) had been feeding three hundred thousand of the poorest of the poor in Kabul. War widows were given special permission to bake the bread. Rules for monitoring the delivery of aid required the WFP to conduct a survey of people entitled to the bread. A WFP official explained the dilemma: "We have to go house to house, and to go house to house we need women, because only women can enter the inner sanctum of Afghan homes. But we're not allowed to hire women." The bakeries were shut down until the WFP agreed to let the Taliban nominate the women to carry out and supervise the survey, reducing its value as an independent audit to zero.

I went to Herat in eastern Afghanistan to report on the drought, and was allowed to film undisturbed on the grounds that my purpose was a humanitarian one. The situation was dire. Thousands of people a day were arriving at a relief camp. Farmers, who only leave their land as a very last resort were among the new arrivals. The camp was in desperate need of food because the regime was making it almost impossible for aid agencies to import and distribute basic supplies.

Oddly, the hotel I stayed at in Herat had one of the two func-
tioning swimming pools in Afghanistan. Only men were allowed
to swim, and even they had to be covered from below the knee to
above the navel. I crouched at a window in a corridor overlooking
the pool, pulled out the camera, and started filming. The pool atten-
dants, members of the religious police known as the Committee for
the Prevention of Vice and the Promotion of Virtue, the Amri Bil
Marouf, carried whips as well as guns. I captured a wonderful scene
in which a young man refused to come down from a diving board
after committing some infraction. When one lifeguard holding a
whip climbed up to get him, the boy jumped and swam to the
other end of the pool. He was chased out by two others, who were
unslinging their AK-47s as they tried to catch him. I was holding
my breath, and trying to steady the camera. I was afraid they would
shoot him, afraid I would be the next target of the Amri Bil Marouf
if anyone saw me, and very much afraid I would laugh out loud,
because the sight of the Mullahs in their beards, turbans, and long
robes running around the pool was so comical. The young man
ran around a corner out of sight, and I could hear the sound of him
being beaten, but not shot.

Taliban fanaticism and incompetence certainly added to the
privations suffered by a long-suffering people during the drought.
Nevertheless, one aspect of Taliban rule that was widely ignored in
the West was that the regime was still quite popular among
Afghans who had welcomed the Taliban takeover in 1996. Many
people were unhappy with the absurd and draconian restrictions
the Taliban imposed, but for the first time in decades, it was possible to travel from one end of the country to the other and expect
that you and your belongings would arrive intact. Farmers could
plant a crop in the spring with a degree of certainty that they would
be able to harvest it in the fall. After years of Soviet occupation,
warlord anarchy, and civil war, in many Afghan eyes, the Taliban's

ability to bring peace and security far outweighed the curtailment of individual rights and liberties.

The international community also neglected to recognize another major Taliban achievement: the eradication of opium poppy cultivation. In 2000, Afghanistan's poppies supplied 70 percent of the world's heroin. The opium crop was about four thousand tonnes. In 2001, the crop was zero. I met the head of the drug-eradication program in Nangarhar Province, Mulvahi Ami Mohammed Hakani, who told me that most farmers obeyed the Taliban edict without question. "All but 5 percent gave up poppies voluntarily," he said. "We put some in prison until they agreed to stop. We did not have to use force, no tanks or anything like that. There were no deaths or injuries." At the time, no farmer dared to disagree, but years later the same farmers told me that they had been compelled to give up the valuable crop, and started growing it again as soon as they were no longer afraid of being shot for doing so.

The United Nations Drug Control Program and the United States Drug Enforcement Agency confirmed the eradication using satellite imagery, but Western governments, disturbed by the Taliban's human-rights record, ignored pleas for a speedy and generous aid program to help Afghan farmers replace their lost livelihood. It was a great opportunity missed.

Having tackled an almost impossible task, and having received nothing whatever in exchange, Taliban leaders decided there was nothing to be gained by accommodating the West. Afghanistan would continue to be ostracized no matter what the government did. The destruction of the Bamiyan Buddhas was one example of the new rebarbative attitude. Another, of far greater consequence, was the presumed deal the Taliban made with Osama bin Laden, sanctioning the September 11 attacks in exchange for the al Qaeda assassination on September 9 of the Taliban's arch-enemy, Ahmad

Shah Masood, leader of the Northern Alliance. I am not arguing that the September 11 attacks would not have happened had the West responded appropriately to the Taliban's eradication of opium. It is certain, though, that after the United States sent cruise missiles into Afghanistan in response to al Qaeda's 1998 attacks on U.S. embassies, the Taliban imposed conditions on bin Laden's continued presence in Afghanistan. At the time the Taliban leader Mullah Omar said, "We told him as a guest that he shouldn't involve himself in any activities that create problems for us. We already have plenty of problems of our own." By 2001, the Taliban's attitude toward bin Laden had changed and it seems reasonable to suppose that their new attitude toward the West had something to do with the shift.

At the end of that trip to cover the drought and opium eradication, I was driving toward the Pakistani border with my Afghan friend Ekram, who was serving as my interpreter, a local camera-man, and the young Taliban official assigned to escort us. We stopped by the side of the road to take a few pictures of people working in the fields. A car drove past, then did a rapid U-turn, and screeched back to where we were filming. Four mullahs jumped out and grabbed us. The mullahs from the Committee for the Prevention of Vice and Promotion of Virtue accused us of try-ing to film women. They grabbed the cassettes I had not had time to hide, and insisted we return with them to Kabul. We were made to check into a hotel and ordered not to leave. The young Taliban official had not been as zealous as he should have been in enforcing the rule on photography. He had stopped us from filming much of the time, but the hope of financial reward had persuaded him to look the other way when we shot discreetly from the van. He had been scared throughout the trip, but now he was terrified. We were to be brought to the Amri bil Marouf office the next day so that the mullahs could look at all the seized cassettes. He was told he would be hanged if a single picture of a woman were found. He knew we had plenty.

During the night, the cameraman fiddled with the contrast of the camera's view-finder so that everything was black, then jammed the control so it could not be adjusted. We told the mullahs that we had scrupulously obeyed the regulations, that we were about to film the landscape, not the farmers, when they arrested us, and that all the seized cassettes were blank. They sat for more than an hour looking through the viewfinder, screening what appeared to be black tapes, and then let us go, with apologies all around.

"Thanks be to God for ignorant officials!" said Ekram.

Three months later, on the evening of September 11, 2001, I was at home in Bangkok, watching an episode of *The Sopranos,* when a friend in China sent me a text message. "Turn on CNN!!!"

Like the rest of the world, I gasped when I saw the second plane hit the World Trade Center towers. Then I called the Marriott Hotel in Islamabad and booked a room overlooking the pool. On that side of the hotel, you could set up a satellite phone antenna aimed at the Indian Ocean satellite. On the other side of the pool, you couldn't use a satellite phone, which meant you had to rely on the hotel switchboard, or run up to the hotel roof and set up the satphone each time you needed it. I knew I was going to need it a lot.

I had no more idea than anyone else who was responsible for the attack on the United States, but I did know that Osama bin Laden was the obvious suspect. Pakistan was the only place to get visas for Afghanistan, as well as the best place to report from while waiting to get into the country. It was a busy two-month-long wait. I attended the frequent anti-American demonstrations, visited the border to talk to truck drivers coming back from Afghanistan, met Afghan exiles, and attended press conferences at the Taliban embassy, which we called "the pirate ship" because of the eye-patches and prosthetic hooks worn by the diplomats, many of whom had been wounded in Afghanistan's long war.

On November 13, we learned that the Taliban had abandoned Kabul to Northern Alliance forces. We raced up to Peshawar in a borrowed SUV to find the Eastern Shura, the parliament of Afghans who had been sitting out the Taliban years in exile in Pakistan, preparing to go home. One leader I knew, a former mujahedeen commander in the war against the Soviet occupation named Engineer Ghaffar, offered to let me join his group. He insisted, though, that I dress as an Afghan. The Pakistani authorities did not allow foreigners into the frontier area, whereas Pashtuns had free passage between the two countries. A friend went to buy clothes and came back with a baby-blue *salwar kameez* tunic, baggy trousers, and a pie-shaped Afghan hat. Feeling more than ridiculous, I pulled a blanket around my head as we headed off toward the Khyber Pass.

We roared up the narrow defiles, a hundred or more SUVs loaded with men and arms, all overtaking one another, and their occupants singing and waving out of the windows. It was after nightfall when we got through the Torkhum Gate and on to Jalalabad.

There were men moving through the darkness in the opposite direction who looked exactly like us, except they weren't carrying guns. They were the Taliban making their negotiated exit. In Jalalabad, an epic meeting of the Eastern Shura began to work out how to divide the spoils: who would be the governor, who the customs collector, who in charge of the highways. It was no trivial matter. The main road was one of the key routes for all goods, licit and illicit, that made their way through Afghanistan in both directions. Jalalabad was a very lucrative choke point, and official positions meant a fortune as well as prestige.

Tribal leaders, warlords, and members of influential families all had descended on Jalalabad to join the returning exiles in the Shura. Bands of gunmen who came with them were riding around in convoys and eyeing one another menacingly. I wanted to get on to the capital as soon as possible. I set up the video-phone and filed some muddy-looking live reports at around day-break, then got ready to leave, only to find that the suv I had borrowed from Islamabad had disappeared. I spent hours looking for the vehicle before one of drivers from the convoy reappeared and explained that he had "borrowed" it to visit relatives. It was late afternoon before we got on the Kabul road. The atmosphere was extremely tense in Jalalabad, and I was glad to leave behind what looked like an impending battle. But I also wanted to travel the road as quickly as possible. I anticipated that it would become much more dangerous once the immediate aftermath of the fall of Kabul had passed.

The Kabul–Jalalabad road was where I had been arrested in June. It also was where the British Empire suffered a catastrophic defeat in 1842 during an uprising against the occupation of Afghanistan. About 16,500 British and Indian troops and civilians, including women and children, set off up the road after surrendering their garrison in Kabul to Afghan forces. According to legend, there was one single survivor, an assistant surgeon named Dr. William Bryden, who rode into the British garrison at Jalalabad, wounded and alone. It was a good story, and the subject of a famous Victorian painting, but there were other survivors: Indian troops, and women, who suffered the unmentionable fate of living with the Afghans who captured them. Dr. Bryden was the lone white male survivor.

The journey, about 150 kilometres, normally takes a few hours, but our journey took much longer because of engine trouble, which made us stop time after time. I had no choice but to travel after dark. There was nowhere safe to stop. We finally made it to Kabul and found a ratty old hotel with a rooftop that I broadcast from at about ten in the evening. The next day four journalists were shot and killed at a roadblock at Sirobi, a town a couple of hours outside Kabul, which we had limped through unmolested the night before.

Afghanistan is essentially a federation of mutually antagonistic ethnic groups who have fought each other vigorously and often, but are, in one sense, curiously united. Afghans of all groups are unanimous in their view that Afghanistan is one country, they belong to it, and it belongs to them. Conflict is never about separation from Afghanistan; it is about how to divide up power and wealth in a state with national borders everyone agrees on. This power-sharing is one of the factors that makes outside intervention so perilous. Foreigners, however well-meaning, cannot possibly acquire the intimate understanding they would need to avoid antagonizing some or all of the groups. Eventually, all outsiders have worn out their welcome.

The morning after I arrived in Kabul, I went over to the foreign ministry to see if I could obtain some sort of credentials. In a city full of armed men, it is always helpful to have an official-looking piece of paper to wave from time to time. Mullah Sharyar had left with the other Taliban leaders, but there behind the desk was his deputy, who had already shaved off his beard. He borrowed my phone to call his brother in Canada, and then gave me an official letter to show to the soldiers at the checkpoints. They mostly were fighters from the north, Tajiks and Uzbecks, who were strangers to the city.

At night, there was gunfire. A city that changes hands is always dangerous until the new masters take control. In Kabul, no one knew yet who the new masters would be. Some old scores were being settled, and some Northern Alliance troops regarded looting as their right. Their officers requisitioned spacious villas and moved in.

In the daytime, there was freedom in the air. Many women threw off their burkas, and in the countryside farmers retrieved the poppy seeds that they had carefully hidden away. The opium-planting season would soon be here, and another war was on its way. Scattered over the brown cityscape and the grey winter sky were small scraps of fluttering colour like a shower of confetti: Thousands of children were flying kites from the flat rooftops. The kites were soaring freely after five years of imprisonment under the Taliban.

I met a group of musicians rehearsing in anticipation of the weddings where they would play again. After the Taliban took over, they had buried their instruments in the backyard. Their faces shone as they made music together after so many years of silence. A cinema was reopened by the projectionist who had hidden the projector and a stash of old movies during the years of darkness.

I also met Saleem Shaheen, an Afghani filmmaker who was shooting the latest of his dreadful rape-and-revenge epics on location in Kabul shortly after the Taliban was overthrown, using a battered old home-video camera to film a pickup cast of family and friends, losing his temper with crowds of curious onlookers, all while playing the hero. "Now this is a pot of goat's head soup if ever I saw one!" he bellowed into the camera, waggling his big black eyebrows. "May God help my mother-in-law rest in peace. She always said you would be a good wife. Your five fingers are like five bright candles, thank you for this delicious food!"

The film, his first in eight years, was about a poor farmer who gets his revenge after being outrageously wronged. He had written the script himself. His last film, made in 1995 when the Taliban was at the gates of Kabul, features a scene in which a rocket lands on a family gathering. The explosion was not a special effect. A Taliban rocket fell on the set, killing nine cast members including the leading actress. Shaheen and his camerman survived. They kept the camera rolling, and used the footage in the movie. "I love you cinema! I love you cinema! I love you too!" he yelled as we said goodbye.

INTERVENTION ALMOST NEVER WORKS OUT as predicted, and it is almost never executed with sufficient thoroughness and commitment. The decision to intervene, either for humanitarian reasons or because a regime has become intolerable, are often made haphazardly, and the results almost always are disappointing. Those decisions deserve care and attention proportional to the blood and treasure lost when bad decisions are made. I have been in Afghanistan many times since the Taliban left. I have watched a growing number of foreign nation-builders and peacekeepers lose their lives in the dusty hills of a country that once again produces 90 percent of the world's heroin.

NATO countries that are still willing to provide troops insist on à la carte deployment, picking and choosing where their forces are deployed and what they do. Countries that have put their troops in harm's way, like Canada and Britain, are naively stirring up a hornet's nest. Pacifying Afghanistan and improving its living standards rapidly would have taken much larger numbers of well-equipped troops, and an intensive and expensive development effort.

In 2005, not long after Canada took responsibility for Kandahar, one of the most difficult regions of the country, I joined the chief of the Defence Staff, General Rick Hillier, on a tour of inspection. Canadians were already taking casualties from roadside bombs and suicide attacks. A few days earlier, an officer had been attacked with an axe and badly injured during a meeting with villagers.

I asked General Hillier if he could identify the little plants that were just beginning to sprout in the fields we were driving through in our heavily armed convoy. Hillier, an intelligent and forthright officer, didn't pretend that he recognized them. He was a little embarrassed to be told we were surrounded on all sides by opium poppies. "You can't stop those kinds of things overnight, and direct action by us would not help that at all," he said.

Employment opportunities are scarce in Afghanistan, and opium is a multi-billion-dollar racket. Even without the ideological and religious opposition of Taliban remnants and other jihadis, the drug trade has created many wealthy and powerful people who have a vested interest in a chaotic country with a weakened government. There also are plenty of young people willing to carry a bomb or a Kalashnikov for a living wage. It doesn't take many of them to tie up thousands of troops.

After 9/11, there really was no choice except to intervene in Afghanistan, but the estimates of what it would take to create a stable democracy there were optimistic to the point of foolishness. In 2004 and 2005, Afghans bravely went out to vote in their first-ever democratic elections. They ended up with a president whose writ runs only as far as Kabul city limits, and a parliament full of drug dealers and warlords who have granted themselves immunity from prosecution for their past crimes. "Many MPs should be sitting in the dock of the International Criminal Court in The Hague charged with war crimes," Malalai Joya, an Independent woman MP told me. "National unity should not be achieved through forgiving national traitors. They must be tried."

———————

"AT FIRST I COULD NOT understand it. As a Chinese, I thought it would be very simple to condemn them, then hang them. Instead, each prisoner was given a lawyer and allowed to defend himself."

Xiao Qian's last assignment, as the only Chinese war correspondent in Western Europe during the Second World War, had been to cover the Nuremberg trials in which Nazi war criminals were tried by the International Military Tribunal.

"The trials were very, very impressive," he said, pausing for thought from time to time. He was recalling the events of fifty years ago with great clarity as we sat in his cluttered study in Beijing. "I think the Russians found it difficult to understand also, but it showed that democracies were different from the Nazis, standing on justice. I was deeply impressed. I think they did the right thing. After all we were fighting not just to win or lose the war; we were fighting for a cause and the Nuremberg trials showed the right spirit."

Xiao Qian was born in 1910, when the last emperor, the young Pu Yi, was still on the throne. He was eighty-five when I interviewed him in 1995. War crimes trials, new in 1945, had become an established part of the international landscape in the intervening years. So had truth commissions, lustration laws, and other mechanisms for nations to begin the painful process of facing up to ugly truths. After the war, the Germans had to create a new word, *vergangenheitsbewältigung*, for their struggle to come to terms with the past, a word they required again after the fall of the Berlin Wall.

Like individuals, countries that do not shine the light of truth into dark corners are condemned to be troubled until they do. It was this belief that persuaded Xiao Qian and many other Chinese intellectuals to respond enthusiastically to the Communist Party's extraordinary campaign for openness and truth in 1957. The People's Republic was only eight years old, but it was clear to everyone that things were not going as well as hoped. The imposition of collective agriculture was creating serious problems in the countryside. There is still debate among historians over whether the Hundred Flowers Movement was a genuine effort to encourage greater public participation in facing these problems and solving them, or a cynical ploy to smoke out critics of the party. Certainly, Xiao Qian believed at the time that Mao Zedong's essay, "On the

Correct Handling of the Contradictions Among the People," which included the classical reference, "Let a hundred flowers bloom, Let a hundred schools of thought contend," was an honest appeal for constructive criticism and suggestions. "I wrote essays for the *People's Daily* and other papers calling for greater tolerance for intellectuals, and freedom from government interference in publishing," Xiao Qian said.

"You really thought it was okay to express yourself freely?"

"Exactly, but actually it was a cynical trap. Some people don't think so, but I feel that way."

The Hundred Flowers Movement was abruptly replaced by the Anti-Rightist Movement in July 1957. By the end of the year, Xiao Qian, and three hundred thousand others who had written articles or sent letters to the government, were denounced and punished as rightists. They were dismissed from their jobs, publicly humiliated as class enemies, imprisoned, or exiled to the countryside. China had begun nineteen years of meltdown, which ended only after the death of Mao Zedong in 1976.

"I was like a ship without a rudder. I didn't know where the country would go, let alone myself," said Xiao Qian. "I was completely lost, but I was not gloomy. I had been the translator of *The Good Soldier Schweik* by Jaroslav Hasek so, like Schweik, I survived by bowing to my persecutors and never contradicting them. Inside, I knew I retained my own judgement, my own mind."

It was Xiao Qian's translation work that had led me to him. He and his wife Wen Jieruo had just published their translation of James Joyce's *Ulysses*, and I was eager to meet the couple who had attempted to make accessible to Chinese readers a novel that is challenging even in its original language. "The most difficult part was Chapter Fourteen," he told me. "It parodies well over a dozen English styles, from Anglo-Saxon down to late nineteenth-century. This was quite impossible. It was beyond our ability to render all these styles, and even if we did, it would be meaningless to our readers. Eventually, we decided to have the more ancient part in semi-classical Chinese, the more colloquial part in journalistic Chinese." Molly Bloom's epic, and at times erotic, train of thought, which runs unpunctuated for the last forty-two pages of the book, is rendered in Beijing street slang.

Xiao Qian's translation is a heroic effort, but ultimately only a partial success. The complex flavours and allusions of Joyce's encyclopedic fusion of a day in the life of a Dublin everyman, and the myth of Ulysses, simply do not translate. Nor did my personal fascination with the challenge of transmitting experiences and ideas from one language and culture to another ever translate into a television report. The cassettes of my interview with Xiao Qian remained on the shelf year after year, until I pulled them down to write about history, truth, and language for this book. From time to time, I would try to interest editors, but whenever I said, "I've got this great interview with the guy who translated *Ulysses* into Chinese," the answer was always a long silence, never "How soon can we get it?"

The first Chinese phrase I learned was *dui bu qi*, which means "excuse me." I needed the phrase to get through the crowds on Tiananmen Square in 1989. Mispronouncing it differently at every attempt, I shouldered and elbowed my way through the millions of protestors, stepping on their feet and bumping them clumsily with my camera tripod, mumbling *deeboochee, doobeecho*, as I sought out English-speaking students to tell me what was going on. When I moved to Beijing shortly after the Tiananmen crisis, the first phrase I had learned proved to be one of the most useful, and also one of the easiest to remember, given the frequency of my blunders, wrong turnings, and misunderstandings of life in China. It's hard to forget a word you have to use many times a day. By the time I moved away again in 1996, my Chinese had improved to the point that I no longer needed to use "excuse me" in every single sentence.

When I came back to live in Beijing for the second time, in 2003, I found that my command of the language had eroded. I was often at a loss for words. Still, I don't think you ever lose a language once you have learned it. Much of what seems at first to be lost forever through long disuse is, in fact, merely submerged. Words and grammar come creeping back to the surface after only a little exposure and practice. Comprehension and speech come back quite quickly, but reading and writing Chinese characters is a unique linguistic challenge that requires daily maintenance. I called up my former Chinese teacher, Li Laoshi, and asked if we could resume our lessons. He had retired some years earlier, and was reluctant at first, remembering, probably, the frustrations of having me for a student.

"I am getting old," he said.

"I have aged, too," I told him. "I might even have matured a little. I'm not as impatient as I used to be. I'm much calmer."

"Really?" he said.

He did not sound convinced, but after a little persuasion, like one of those ageing bank robbers in the opening scenes of a caper movie, he finally agreed to come out of retirement for one last job. We met for an hour, three mornings a week, to study the Chinese idioms known as *cheng yu*, set phrases usually four characters long that are the motherlode of thousands of years of literature, philosophy, history, wit, and wisdom. Li Laoshi's lessons are a rambling exploration of Chinese language, thought, and experience. One expression leads to another, which reminds him of a third, which explains a fourth, which, he suggests, some misguided students might mispronounce, unless they carefully study a fifth, which cannot be overlooked.

He became my teacher in the days when China's "Regulations Concerning Foreign Journalists" required us to hire all staff, including language teachers, from the government's Diplomatic Service Bureau. I asked for a teacher who could speak neither English nor French, because I wanted to learn Chinese in Chinese from the beginning.

At first, it is a confusing and frustrating way to learn a new language, but it forced me to listen and think in a new way. It was my good fortune that when Li became a teacher, China lost a great actor. Unable to give the English equivalent of a new expression, he became a marvellous performer. He used minute adjustments of his features, gestures, and glances to become a jealous neighbour, a greedy banker, or a pompous official as he explained the most abstract vocabulary, illustrating with examples from his own life, today's news, or both. "It's like what happened in New Orleans during the hurricane," he told me, when I asked about a word in a story from China's Warring States period a couple of thousand years ago.

"A kind of stealing?" I asked, checking my guess that the word probably meant looting or ransacking.

"Yes. Taking everything and leaving emptiness behind. There was a report about New Orleans on the TV news," he said.

"It usually happens in a war?" I asked, attempting to fine-tune my understanding.

"Exactly. Looting. I did it once," he said with a grin. Li Laoshi was brought up in Dalian, in northeast China, during the Japanese occupation. "I was about six or seven years old at the time. I was going home one day toward the end of the war, when I got swept up in a big crowd outside a Japanese army storage depot. The people in front broke into the building, and we all rushed inside. Everyone began to grab anything they could carry. I didn't really have any idea of what might be valuable, but I didn't want to be left out. I managed to snatch a box of biscuits."

The elderly teacher was transformed before my eyes into a

small boy clutching an imaginary box of biscuits in his arms, glancing over his shoulder as he gleefully rushed home with his loot. "My granddad gave me such a whack! He beat me half to death, because the Japanese would have chopped my head off if they caught me." He brandishes an imaginary samurai sword. "He was right. In those days, the Japanese would kill Chinese like flies, without a second thought. Not long after that the Russians came, and I saw them kill so many Japanese the same way."

He pushes the lesson home: "The Russians did lots of looting too. 'Looting!' Please remember this word and how to use it. See you next week."

Li Laoshi talks about the old days a lot, but there are some old days he never talks about. He will occasionally start illustrating a word with a reminiscence from the 1960s or 1970s, and then suddenly clam up, as he remembers his experiences in the Anti-Rightist Movement, the Great Leap Forward, and the Great Proletarian Cultural Revolution. He has never told me the details of what happened to him, and I doubt that he ever will. The humiliation and resentment show plainly on his face, but he is too proud to share his memories with me.

During the chaos of Mao's last ten years, everything broke down. Schools and universities were closed, and people tore one another to pieces in an orgy of denunciation and violence. No one was untouched. When the Cultural Revolution was finally over, the verdict was delivered that Mao Zedong had been 70 percent right, 30 percent wrong. The Gang of Four, led by Mao's harridan of a wife, Jiang Qing, were safely locked up, and Deng Xiaoping consolidated his hold on power. A literary genre called "wound literature" emerged. Writing about victimization became acceptable, but an objective assessment of responsibility, a truthful account of who did what to whom, and why and how it happened, is an unattainable dream.

Zhang Rong, who writes under the pen name Jung Chang, introduced wound literature to Western readers with her best-selling memoir *Wild Swans*. The book is about the women of three generations of her family: herself, her mother, and her grand-mother. She described her parents as upstanding local officials devoted to the welfare of the people, who were ousted and merci-lessly persecuted by wicked rivals taking advantage of the chaos. Everywhere in China, the twists and turns of political campaigns were used as the pretext for power grabs, the settlement of old scores, the pursuit of neighbourhood feuds, and for violent conflicts between rival gangs and militias.

When I travelled to Sichuan to make a program about the return home of Zhang Rong, who by then had become a world-famous writer who lived in London, I met and interviewed several of the people she had written about, including her mother. While I admired the book, and thought it was a valuable contribution to Western understanding of China, I had always suspected her ver-sion of events was a bit of a whitewash where her family was con-cerned. It seemed their motives were always positive, their actions selfless and generous, in contrast to the evil scheming of their black-hearted rivals. A lot of what happened during the Cultural Revolution was human nature run riot, "outs" replacing "ins," and "downs" attacking "ups," only to find their roles reversed with the next wave of hysteria. My meeting with Zhang Rong's mother, and with some of the neighbours, confirmed what I had suspected. She was not a saint. She was, as one of them put it, "a lamp that does not save on oil," or in English, "a piece of work." Her behaviour was neither much better, nor much worse, than anyone else's during that turbulent time.

When the communist system collapsed in Eastern Europe in 1989, I was rather surprised not to see corpses hanging on lamp-posts from the Baltic to the Black Sea. In communist countries, snitches and schoolyard bullies rise to positions of authority. The factory foreman, the cop on the beat, your child's school principal, the woman behind the meat counter, or just about anyone with an ounce of power, can arbitrarily make your life miserable. The relatively low incidence of vengeance can only be explained by an overall feeling of complicity. Almost everyone behaved badly in one way or another, so that they and their families could survive.

It is usually the victims who reveal the most about political persecution. The perpetrators are not so forthcoming. Xu Liangying, best known as Albert Einstein's translator in China, has the look of a man who could be the conscience of a nation, but he has things on his conscience, too. Professor Xu has a deeply furrowed face, like the ancient mariner's, and a shock of white hair. He is happy to talk about the past, but he's not always available. When the authorities think he has been talking too much, or will talk too much, the door to his apartment building is blocked by police and no one is allowed to see him. Like a flock of swallows arriving with the change of seasons, the police show up at Professor Xu's door in late spring to prevent him from giving interviews as the anniversary of the Tiananmen massacre approaches. I first visited him in March 1993, well in advance of the sensitive anniversary. Hanging on the wall of Professor Xu's book-lined study was a portrait of Albert Einstein, with a quotation, "Great spirits have always encountered violent opposition from mediocre minds."

"China has a long history of punishing people for their words," he says in his heavy Zhejiang accent. "It has to stop."

As a young man, Xu Liangying had two passions: physics and revolution. He resolved to become a physicist after reading a book of Einstein's essays called *The World as I See It*. He joined the communist movement in the belief that revolution was the only solution to China's terrible poverty. Professor Xu's conscience is troubled by his assignment at the Academy of Sciences after the communist victory in 1949. He was the Academy's chief censor, in charge of examining scientific papers to sniff out signs of counter-revolutionary thinking. "It was a bad deed," he says. "Science is a search for truth. It should be pursued for its own sake without political interference."

Like Xiao Qian, the man who opened one of the greatest twentieth-century, English-language novels for Chinese readers, Xu Liangying was purged in 1957. He was branded, not just a rightist, but an extreme rightist. His wife was forced to divorce him, and he was exiled to the countryside. Rehabilitated after Mao's death, and later remarried to his wife, Professor Xu was in trouble again in early 1989.

After a decade of the Gaige Kaifang Reform and Opening policies introduced by Deng Xiaoping, he became convinced that economic reform must be accompanied by political change as a necessary ingredient in the modernization of China. His passion for physics and revolution had evolved into a passion for physics and democracy. He pointed out that Hitler and Stalin both had insisted on bending science and truth to suit their perverse political theories. "In the 1930s and 1940s, Nazi Germany fanatically purged so-called 'Jewish science.' In the 1940s and 1950s, the Soviet Union liquidated Morganian genetics, criticized Einstein's theories of cosmology and relativity, and so forth," he wrote. "In the 1950s through the 1970s, China witnessed successive academic criticism campaigns and political movements. The reasons why the two great socialist countries would surprisingly follow in the footsteps of Nazi Germany, inflicting heart-rending stupidities on ourselves, were that politically, there has been no democracy, and that the people lack democratic civil consciousness."

These outspoken views were part of the intellectual ferment that culminated in the student protests in the spring of 1989, and their violent suppression. Since then, Professor Xu has joined with relatives of those killed and other intellectuals in publishing open letters and petitions, demanding that the government conduct an honest review of its verdict that the protests were "counter-revolutionary turmoil," and that the use of military force was necessary and correct. "To talk about modernization without mentioning human rights is like climbing a tree to catch a fish," they wrote in 1994.

In 1999, as he was approaching his eightieth birthday, Professor Xu wrote another long open letter arguing that China should follow Taiwan's example and eventually introduce multi-party politics and free elections. "For the authorities this is a feasible and admirable path to take. Otherwise," he warned, "it is unlikely they will be able to escape the fate of Marcos in the Philippines and Suharto in Indonesia." He said that China has had enough of revolution. "After twelve years of war and nineteen years of self-destruction, China cannot withstand further turmoil," he wrote. Implicitly, he was criticizing those who advocated radical direct action — including some of the student leaders in 1989 — of merely repeating the mistake that Mao had made. "Political power obtained through violent means simply results in a new dictatorship and yet another feudal change of dynasties."

"We need to do this slowly and prudently," he told me. "This is going to be a long journey."

China still has not recovered from the effects of two fanatical decades. Tens of millions of lives were lost in the greatest famine in human history. Tens of millions of people, who might have made incalculable contributions, wasted their best years in prison or labouring in the countryside. The reverberations of years without education are still being felt.

"You talk about waste! Something you cannot imagine. In the early 1950s, we became mad wanting to catch up to America in a few years, but we lost no end of valuable things," said translator Xiao Qian. "I was very, very bitter. But people I knew were beaten to death, or lost one of their limbs or became blind, so later I had a strange feeling of being lucky, because I could easily have been one of those people."

"There is a queer logic, very enigmatic," he said. "Had I not been branded a rightist in 1957, my fate would be much worse, very likely I would not be alive today. In 1966 anyone who wrote anything, even historical plays, would be branded a class enemy and imprisoned, and many were murdered. Since I was a class enemy in 1957, I was not allowed to write anything. So when the Cultural Revolution came, my account was blank. So you see my fate in 1957 was luck in disguise."

Translators work to enrich a culture; censors work to impoverish it. Translators add ideas and human experience to the great river of thought available in a language; political fanatics try to dam the river and turn it into a stagnant pool. These measures can work for a while, but somehow the river always manages to burst its banks. The greatest glory of China is its language, which transcends the borders of the Middle Kingdom and its current rulers. It resides in Chinese societies in Taiwan, Singapore, and Hong Kong, and in the Chinese diaspora in every city in the world. It stretches back in an unbroken stream for thousands of years. The ruler of the day, whether it is Emperor Qin Shiu Huang, who burned books and murdered scholars in the third century B.C., or Mao Zedong, who confined artistic expression to eight model revolutionary operas in the twentieth century, can restrict what people say and do, but can never restrict what people think.

When he is asked about his suicide attempt in 1968, Xiao Qian simply does not answer. Instead, he finds enough evidence in a turbulent lifetime for an optimistic conclusion. "However bad, barbaric, and reactionary a regime can be, it cannot turn the clock of history backwards. I realized that from the Second World War. Hitler and Mussolini certainly wanted to enslave the world, but after the war, the world jumped forward. The colonies all were liberated. I have confidence in history."

· 7 ·

DARKNESS

"God help all poor souls lost in the dark."

— ROBERT BROWNING

Monday afternoons in Beijing often find me at the clinical psychology ward on the second floor of a hospital in Haidian district, visiting the alcoholics being treated there. Most weeks there are about a dozen people in the ward's little classroom, half of them patients, half former patients who are now living sober lives in the community.

Back in the 1990s, a number of foreign alcoholics living in Beijing met several times with Chinese doctors and officials in the health ministry to see if we could be allowed to meet with Chinese alcoholics, but we were always rebuffed. "We don't have alcoholism like you do in the West," one doctor told me. "If Chinese drink too much, it's because they have had hard lives and because of our culture of drinking at banquets. Chinese people don't like to talk about their problems the way you do, and they keep it in the family." This is an excuse you hear all over the world, just as problem drinkers everywhere believe their "unique" circumstances give them a justification for continuing to drink.

The real reason the Chinese doctors turned us away was that

any activity involving unsupervised contact between foreigners and Chinese was regarded with deep suspicion. Medical professionals feared that the *youguan bumen* — "the relevant departments" — usually meaning the police and security bureaus, would frown on what we were proposing. No doctor was willing to take responsibility for allowing us to become involved with the treatment of alcoholics for fear of getting into trouble with those relevant departments. In the long history of China, the search for someone to blame has never begun with, "Who kept those foreigners out?" But it has often started with, "Who the hell allowed those foreigners in?"

Finally, in 2000, two Chinese doctors came back from a visit to the United States infected with the idea that when alcoholics try to help each other, they sometimes succeed where doctors and nurses fail. Those two doctors bravely decided to let the foreigners in. Their courage was rewarded when two of their chronic, hopeless cases, frequent visitors to the detox unit, began to get well after starting to meet with foreign alcoholics. As more Chinese alcoholics gradually followed in their footsteps, the relevant departments did take a close look at what was going on. The doctors helped to allay suspicion that the foreigners had religious or political motives. In this way, what had been unthinkable became tolerable, and Chinese alcoholics now are allowed to organize their own meetings and run their own programs independently of the hospitals. This was a tolerant and enlightened decision. It was also a decision that reflected the ambiguous nature of change in China, a country that is moving in the direction of a more open society at the same time as it continues to lock up people for protesting injustice.

The key principle of recovery from alcoholism is rigorous honesty, and the key way of putting that principle into practice is by admitting the truth about ourselves to others. It is not something that comes naturally to people who have been conditioned by years of political meetings where conformity is the only safe policy. Anyone who grew up in the People's Republic learned to digest and regurgitate stock phrases, and to use them to conceal their true thoughts and feelings.

When Chinese alcoholics first arrive at the hospital, they tend either to say nothing at all, or things like, "I will study the foreign visitor and try to improve myself under your wise guidance." Sometimes, after listening for a while, they say, "You know, I drink the same way you used to."

Talking to them is just like talking to alcoholics anywhere in the world. They do drink the same way I used to, and for the same reasons, and they get into the same scrapes, and do the same damage to those close to them. By recognizing this truth, and by abandoning excuses and rationalizations and the belief that being a Chinese drunk is somehow different from being a foreign one, they come to a turning point on the road to recovery.

None of us has a magic cure for alcoholism, but our first-hand experience gives us unique credibility with active drinkers. It is like having a light to shine into a dark room, so the people trapped inside can understand things in a way they could not before. When it is successful, it is an amazing thing, but the addiction to alcohol is persistent, and many sufferers cannot or will not see their way out.

The regimes in some countries, too, become blind to the benefits change may bring to their people. "Back in the 1950s, people here were better off than we were," mused the Chinese businessman as he looked out of the train window at a group of North Korean peasants receding into the distance at a steady ten kilometres an hour. We were sharing a compartment on the train from the Chinese border to the North Korean capital a few weeks before North Korea's nuclear test in 2006. I was trying to make a short documentary while posing as a businessman. Lao Wang was a real businessman on his way to Pyongyang on behalf of the trading company he works for. "Coming here is like time travel, going back to the China of the 1970s," he said, "but basically people here are well-educated and competent. The problem is a political one. If they could solve that, everything would be fine."

North Korea's political problem is unique. The place it reminds me of most is Romania under Nicolae Ceauşescu, where an entire nation was supposed to spend its time singing the praises of "Alexander of the Carpathians" by the light of a single forty-watt bulb. In the Democratic People's Republic of Korea, the hymns of praise are to the "Lodestar of the Twenty-First Century," "Great Master of Leadership," "Great Thinker and Theoretician," and "Dear Leader" Kim Jong Il, and his father, the "Great Leader" Kim Il Sung. Kim Il Sung died in 1994, but he remains head of state in perpetuity. Inside a vast marble mausoleum in Pyongyang, eerie funeral dirges accompany the tens of thousands of pilgrims a day, who ride silently on long moving sidewalks to view his embalmed remains.

The cult of personality surrounding the only two leaders North Korea has ever had, one dead and one alive, is beyond parody. All visitors to Pyongyang are taken first to a giant statue of The Great Leader Kim Il Sung, where they are expected to lay wreaths and be filmed by the television crew that is constantly on duty. It is difficult to refuse without causing offence and jeopardizing the rest of your visit, so somewhere on file at the national TV station are several cassettes containing pictures of me performing reluctant homage — pictures, I fear, that could one day come back to haunt me if an unfriendly broadcaster were to get hold of them. Similarly, many foreign ministry archives, including the one in Pyongyang, contain grovelling letters I have written when applying for visas that would also be extremely embarrassing if they were ever published.

My first visit to North Korea was in 1995 to cover an event that was grandly called the International Sports and Cultural Festival for Peace. It turned out to be a professional wrestling bout organized by a Japanese wrestler with good connections in Pyongyang, who judged, rightly, that defeating an American named Ric Flair in the North Korean capital would go down well with the wrestling audience. In the days leading up to the match, we were taken to umpteen monuments to the glorious achievement of the Kims, and to the Children's Palace, where child virtuosos with creepy fixed grins performed lavish musical tributes. Everywhere we went, officially designated "ordinary people" pretended to do ordinary things. When we arrived at the model department store, the customers and clerks snapped to attention, and began pretending to buy and sell things. At the hospital, doctors in white coats with razor-sharp creases pretended to examine patients wearing starched pyjamas. In the national library, the Grand People's Study House, readers bent over books and made reverential notes from some of the thirty million volumes, vast numbers of them by or about the leaders, Great and Dear.

Every visit to Pyongyang includes at least some return visits to those same places. It is extraordinarily difficult to visit a place where real people do ordinary things, and talking to such people is absolutely out of the question. Whatever I have managed to do in North Korea, either with an official journalist's visa, or under various other pretexts, does not exactly count as journalism. Every foreigner who tries to do anything in North Korea, whether it is reporting, running an aid program, or conducting business, has to make compromises just to get through the door. One does what one can. By 2006, back in the Grand People's Study House for the third or fourth time, I found that a computer room had been added to the marble halls. I asked our guide, Ms. Kim, if the terminals were connected to the Internet.

"Only inside our country," she said.

The people hunched over the terminals were studying the works of the Great Leader and the Dear Leader.

"In the near future we will connect to the Internet," Ms. Kim added.

"Do you have a date for that?" I asked.

"In the near future, in the near future," said Ms. Kim.

Only trusted senior officials have email addresses. Personal computers are unheard of, and one thing you cannot do on a visit to North Korea is call home. Cellphones are confiscated at the border.

As our train clattered through the countryside, Lao Wang and I watched peasants work their fields by hand, with scarcely a tractor in sight. He told me he thought North Korea could quickly replicate China's economic miracle if only it abandoned its Stalinist political system. He said businessmen and politicians in China's industrial northeast have big plans for a network of superhighways linking China, through North Korea, to new ports on the Pacific, as well as to the markets and technology of South Korea. He believed that if there were political change in North Korea, northeastern China, home to a large talent pool of ethnic Koreans, would, along with South Korea, play a role similar to the one Hong Kong played in the 1990s, providing investment and skills for China's transformation. "We could do it very quickly if the political problems were solved. I don't think North Korea can be like this for very much longer," he said.

China has been trying to persuade Kim Jong Il to follow its example of economic reform ever since he took over North Korea on the death of his father in 1994. China's leaders hope to entice him into the sort of Marxist-Leninist reforms that have worked so well for them. Whenever he visits China, he is taken on high-tech tours of the parts of China where the neon shines brightest. But there is one great flaw in this approach. Change in China began only after Mao Zedong's death, when it became possible to admit that the Great Helmsman may have been wrong about a few things. There is no way for a regime like Kim's to both loosen up and remain in power. Kim Jong Il's surreal cult of personality guarantees that North Korea is not a candidate for gradual reform. To many outsiders, Kim is a pudgy figure of fun, with a bad haircut and high-heeled shoes, but in fact he is a ruthless, astute, and successful dictator who sees nuclear weapons as his only guarantee of survival, and any loosening of his grip as suicidal.

As Lao Wang and I passed through small-town train stations, we could see evidence of North Korea's rudimentary market economy. The platforms were full of shabbily dressed peasants waiting for a train to take them to the city. Every peasant's back was bent under the weight of a bag, a box, or a bundle, full of produce for sale in the small free markets that form on street corners in Pyongyang.

Like many Chinese caught up in the pressure and hurly-burly of twenty-first-century business, Lao Wang looked back on China's years of orthodox Maoism with more than a touch of nostalgia, which blurred his perceptions of North Korea. "There's no pressure, no competition," he said. "In the 1970s you just went to work and ate your meals. It was really relaxed."

Perhaps so, but China's Maoist years created the worst famine in the history of the world. The isolation of North Korea, and its insistence on applying the crackpot theory of socialist self-reliance known as *juche*, has reduced most ordinary Koreans to abject poverty. Estimates of the number of North Koreans who died in the famines of the 1990s range from half a million to three million. Human Rights Watch considers one million to be a reasonable estimate. The World Food Programme says simply that there are no reliable figures. Millions of North Koreans depend on WFP rations for their basic nutrition. At one point, the WFP was feeding a third of

North Korea's population, and yet the Democratic People's Republic of Korea is a grudging and capricious recipient of the world's generosity. The state makes life difficult for aid officials, with arbitrary regulations and stringent limits on what they can see, where they can go, and who they can hire. After having their operations shut down entirely on one occasion, WFP officials spent months pleading to be allowed to return, an odd case of the rich begging to be allowed to help the destitute.

In agreeing to North Korea's conditions, United Nations agencies commit breaches in UN rules, and allow financial irregularities that even UN auditors, who normally take an extremely lenient view of their colleagues' behaviour, have found unacceptable. The auditors, refused entry into North Korea, have been unable to verify controls on tens of millions of dollars in disbursements by UN agencies, which make all kinds of payments directly to the North Korean government in hard currency. WFP officials insist they make every effort to ensure that the millions of tons of food aid provided do actually feed hungry North Koreans, and are not diverted to feed the million-strong armed forces. They point out that aid comes in the form of grain, whereas under the regime's "army first" policy, the army has priority over local resources, and receives all it wants of the preferred staple, rice, before civilians get any. The UN's justification for helping a regime that is willing to let its people starve while maintaining a vast army and building nuclear weapons, and accepting whatever unreasonable conditions that regime lays down, is simply the "humanitarian imperative." No matter how distasteful the regime, the world must help the hungry.

I have noticed over the years that North Korean officials are becoming increasingly corrupt and cynical. Every orthodox communist country has a hard-currency black market, and officials in many countries have asked me for bribes in U.S. dollars, often disguised as overtime payments or facility fees. This did not used to be the case in North Korea, but recently, requests for handouts have become routine. Officials now ask for euros, however, since North Korea began punishing the United States by refusing dollars in 2002.

In 2003, on a visit to Rajin-Sonbong, where North Korea has tried unsuccessfully to attract investors to a special economic zone close to the joint borders of North Korea, China, and Russia, I was woken by a late-night knock on my door. It is traditional in communist countries for a knock on the door after midnight to be followed by an unpleasant surprise, so I took the time to put my videocassettes and notes back in their hiding places before opening up. I need not have bothered. It was only Mr. Kim with his hand out again.

Mr. Kim, the senior trade official responsible for organizing our trip, had a habit of shamelessly asking for money at odd moments, and on odd pretexts, without ever being so vulgar as to remind me out loud that he could easily turn organization into disorganization if he chose to do so. Shuffling his feet outside my door, he explained in exquisite old-fashioned English that he was in sudden difficulties with his blood pressure, and needed a hundred euros to buy medicine. I invited him in for a chat. I felt it would be impolite to pour scorn on his chances of finding a twenty-four-hour pharmacy, or to inquire why medicine was not provided gratis in a country so wisely guided by the Dear Leader, or to refuse his request point-blank. Instead, I changed the subject and asked whether his excellent English had led to much travel outside North Korea. "Oh! Yes, indeed! I am exceedingly well-travelled," he answered, with an enigmatic smile. "I wonder if you might guess where?" "China?" I suggested. "Yes," he said, "and Pakistan and Iran. On many occasions. Look how late it is! I have to leave. Good night."

As I walked him to the elevator, Mr. Kim easily deflected my persistent questions about Abdul Qadeer Khan, Pakistan's proliferator-in-chief, the man who sold nuclear know-how to North Korea, Libya, and Iran, with a few remarks about tomorrow's weather. Since that night, I have often wondered whether I let the scoop of the decade slip through my fingers. What nuclear secrets might Mr. Kim have revealed in exchange for a handful of euros?

Of course, the people of any country are to some extent responsible for whatever mess their country gets into, but the dangerous muddle on the Korean peninsula is also the culmination of an inordinate amount of outside intervention. Japan, the United States, Russia, China, and the United Nations all bear their share of responsibility for the miserable plight of the North Korean people and the grotesque nuclear standoff that threatens us all.

Koreans on both sides of the border describe themselves as sharing a national cultural trait, an emotion known as *han*. It combines resentment and pride. Some Koreans have suggested that it has its roots in the rigid hierarchies of traditional Korean society. Others believe that the feelings of oppression, injustice, isolation, and deep sadness embodied in *han* stem from a conviction that Korea's inherent superiority and great destiny have been stifled by the country's unfortunate geographical location, between two aggressive and more powerful neighbours, China and Japan.

Japan annexed Korea in 1910, and maintained a brutal and oppressive colonial occupation there until the end of the Second World War. The United States and the Soviet Union agreed at the Yalta conference to divide the peninsula into two occupation zones at the 38th Parallel, and each installed a puppet regime on its own side of the line — Kim Il Sung on the Soviet side, Syngman Rhee on the American side. Each of the two strongmen, proxies for the rival ideologies of the Cold War, was intent on reuniting Korea under his own rule. Kim launched the Korean War by invading South Korea in 1950.

The capricious nature of international interventions, and their moral relativity, are well illustrated by the meetings of the United Nations Security Council, which passed resolutions 82 through 85 between June 25 and July 3, 1950. The UN voted to go to war, calling on members to join a force under the command of the United States. The resolutions taking the UN into a civil war were possible only because the Soviet Union was boycotting the international organization. The Soviet delegation was not present to cast a veto. Significantly, the reason for the Soviet boycott was that the People's Republic of China, founded in 1949, was being prevented from taking up its UN seat by American support for the rival Chinese Nationalists, who had lost their civil war and retreated to Taiwan. The United States managed to keep the world's most populous country out of the UN until 1971.

UN decisions to intervene, not to intervene, to apply sanctions, to limit sanctions, or to lift them, are all more or less haphazard. They are made according to the geopolitical weather patterns of the day, rather than adhering to clearly understood moral principles. Any international body seeking to make decisions in an atmosphere of conflicting national interests is bound to be flawed, but the UN's record of sins, of commission and omission, of ill-conceived action or inaction where action was clearly a moral obligation, is nevertheless a breathtaking one.

By October 1950, the United Nations force was winning the Korean War and advancing steadily north. Despite orders from Washington to be extremely cautious in even approaching the Chinese border, let alone crossing it, the American commander, General Douglas MacArthur, was keen to extend the war into China, for the same reason that later American generals in Vietnam extended their war into Cambodia — to deny their enemies supply routes. According to cables between Mao Zedong and Josef Stalin, the Chinese feared the worst: They assumed that once a UN force led by the United States had effective control of the entire Korean peninsula, an attack on China would surely follow. Mao ordered a pre-emptive strike. More than a quarter of a million Chinese soldiers crossed into North Korea, forcing the United Nations troops into a headlong retreat. The UN counter attacked and eventually, two-and-a-half years and more than a million lives later, the two sides fought to a stalemate along the 38th Parallel where it all started. An armistice was signed in 1953, but there has never been a peace treaty. Technically, North Korea and the United Nations are still at war, but North Korea has enjoyed more than half a century of immunity from further international action, except for a few sanctions. Perpetual negotiations are a small price to pay for a free hand.

By any objective standard, North Korea is a rogue regime. It murders and starves its own people; it traffics in drugs and counterfeit currency; it has committed numerous documented acts of international terrorism; it has acquired nuclear technology and conducted a credible nuclear test after signing agreements promising not to do so; and it confounds the world's ability to devise an effective strategy to bring about any change whatsoever in its behaviour.

Asia's other untouchable rogue is Burma, under military rule since 1962.

There was a brief window of opportunity for decisive change in Burma in 1990, which I didn't recognize when I saw it. Nor did the opponents of the ruling Burmese generals. I had arrived in the Burmese capital, Rangoon, in early June — late for the election which had been held on May 27. I had been shuttling between India and Pakistan, which had been indulging in one of their periodic visits to the brink of war. At the time, Burma was regarded as something of a journalistic backwater. Nevertheless, the elections had turned out to be much more interesting than anyone predicted. Final results were not in when I arrived, but it was clear that the National League for Democracy (NLD) led by Aung San Suu Kyi had won a landslide victory. Even though the election was over, I had decided to take advantage of a visa, which had been difficult to get, to go see what would happen next. The answer was: nothing.

I spent a week in Rangoon trying to find people to talk to, but government offices and the offices of the NLD were deserted. It was as if everyone, shocked by the result, had gone home to wait until someone told them what to do. Aung San Suu Kyi herself had been under house arrest since halfway through the campaign, and the closest we got to her was to drive by her house on University Avenue, secretly taking pictures of the sandbagged military checkpoints outside.

There were secret police everywhere, and one of their primary tasks was to stop foreigners from taking pictures. The first time they arrested me, I had no idea who they were. Two men simply walked up beside me without speaking. One made an almost imperceptible gesture — he tapped his shoulder with two fingers — and was surprised when I did not immediately stop what I was doing. I later learned that the gesture, evoking a military epaulette, means "you're busted." In Burma, it is universally understood and instantly obeyed. I have seen it at one time or another on almost every trip since.

A hundred years ago, Burma exported two million tons of rice a year. Today, it can barely feed itself. One of the richest jewels in the crown of the British Empire is now one of the poorest countries in Asia. When it was divesting itself of its empire, Britain made a botch of preparing many of its former colonies for independence, but Burma, with its extremely complex population mix of more than 135 distinct ethnic groups, is an outstanding failure. A former postal clerk-turned-general, who changed his name from Shu Maung to Ne Win, meaning "as bright as the sun," seized power in 1962 and imposed what he called "the Burmese Way to Socialism" for the next twenty-six years. Superstitious and autocratic, lacking any shred of economic common sense, he beggared the nation. A typical economic decree scrapped the national currency overnight, and issued new notes in multiples of nine. I was nonplussed at the airport, when changing a compulsory amount of dollars at the absurdly low official rate, to be paid out in notes in denominations of nine and forty-five kyats.

In hindsight, it seems to me that if everyone in Rangoon who was sick to death of military rule had marched to Aung San Suu Kyi's house on election day in 1990, they could possibly have liberated her and claimed their election victory. Mass demonstrations claiming victory, and a refusal to take no for an answer might have prevailed over a demoralized, confused, and indecisive junta. Two years had passed since the army's violent suppression of an uprising led by students in 1988, and the generals had staged the election in the mistaken belief that voters would endorse their rule. Taken by surprise by the result, they might have bowed to the will of the people — if the people had shown a willingness to go all the way. In the event, the opposition, which won 392 of 489 seats, sat back and waited for the military regime, the State Law and Order Restoration Council (SLORC), to work out that the elections had been a mistake and refuse to implement the results.

Aung San Suu Kyi had become Burma's opposition leader during the 1988 uprising, when she stepped up to the microphone to make her first-ever public speech to half-a-million people gathered under the beautiful golden spires of the Shwedagon Pagoda on August 26, 1988. Earlier that year, as public protests against the Ne Win dictatorship had gathered pace, she had taken a break from her life in Britain with her husband, an Oxford academic, and her two sons, to return to Rangoon to care for her dying mother. Her father, Aung San, leader of the battle for independence from Britain, had been assassinated by a rival politician in 1947, when Aung San Suu Kyi was two.

Ne Win had already resigned in July 1988, and a full-scale uprising was launched by students and monks on August 8. When she joined the movement on August 26, Aung San Suu Kyi told the huge crowd that the protests were "Burma's second struggle for independence." She invoked her father's name, and pledged to participate in the "struggle for freedom." While her father's name alone was enough to unite the movement behind her, Aung San Suu Kyi is also a commanding public speaker and beautiful woman with enormous charisma. She was quickly acclaimed as the opposition leader.

In the weeks that followed the 1988 uprising, the generals declared a coup, shuffled their feet, changed their leadership, and then struck. Thousands were killed in a brutal campaign of repression that lasted into October. Aung San Suu Kyi was arrested at the beginning of the crackdown, and began her long years in and out of house arrest in her family's crumbling home beside Inya Lake.

I finally met Aung San Suu Kyi in 2000, after a friendly Western diplomat helped to arrange an interview. My colleagues and I smuggled the cameras into a safe house in Rangoon the day before the meeting. This was during a brief interlude in her long house arrest. She was allowed to leave her home, although her movements were still extremely restricted.

Aung San Suu Kyi arrived wearing, as always, a flower in her hair. Five-feet, four-inches tall, she has an aura of imperturbable Buddhist composure, and a will of steel. "What we want is for the international community to indicate clearly that an illegal regime which has taken over the power of government by force should not be encouraged to stay on and oppress the people," she told me.

During our conversation, she returned time after time to the idea that the international community has a responsibility to bring about change in Burma. I asked her about the decision by some Western countries to co-operate with the regime in the hope of combatting the drug trade. "If they really want to stop the production of drugs in Burma, then they have to do something about instituting a responsible, accountable government in Burma, because simply co-operating with this regime is like treating the symptoms of the disease rather than its root cause," she replied.

She rejects the common argument that engagement is a more effective way to bring about change than treating a country as a pariah and applying sanctions. "This constructive-engagement game has been played in Burma by several countries, and it has not really got us anywhere. I think we can say constructive engagement has damaged the cause of democracy."

I am rarely uncomfortable during interviews, but during this one I was on edge. I tried diplomatically to raise the subject of Aung San Suu Kyi's children, whom she is never allowed to see, and her husband, Michael Aris, who had died two years before. Knowing he was dying of cancer, he had applied for a visa to visit her in Rangoon. In an act of mean-spirited spite, the regime refused, and offered instead to allow Aung San Suu Kyi to leave for Britain. She declined, knowing that she would never be allowed to return.

"You have made many personal sacrifices . . ." I began gingerly.

"I never comment on personal matters," she interrupted, gazing calmly into my eyes. I knew nothing could help me to find the courage to probe further.

I have rarely met anyone who combines such a profound sense of duty, sacrifice, and destiny, with an unshakeable conviction that she is doing the right thing. "Oh yes, we will prevail, there is no doubt about it," she told me as I left.

Aung San Suu Kyi is committed to non-violence, and many Burmese follow her lead. In August 2007, when small protests sparked by rising fuel prices turned into mass demonstrations led by Buddhist monks against the regime, the army again opened fire without hesitation, and the protests subsided. Military rule is so entrenched in Burma, that it is hard to see what, aside from a new, more determined uprising, can change it.

Although certain groups have been engaged in armed resistance to successive regimes in Rangoon since the Second World War, opponents of the generals have never been united. Aung San Suu Kyi's father, Aung San, and other leaders of the independence movement together known as the "thirty comrades," had been armed and trained by Japan, and they had fought with Japan's occupying army for most of the Second World War. Meanwhile, the British armed and trained guerrilla units recruited from the ethnic minorities in Burma to fight against the Japanese. After the war was over, some of the ethnic minorities that had fought on the British side regarded the constitutional arrangements Britain negotiated with the Burmese nationalists, under Aung San, as a betrayal of the promises of future autonomy they had been given. They had the weapons and training, so they just kept on fighting, refusing to co-operate with the newly independent Union of Burma unless they were given the right to run their own affairs.

Delia Sie belongs to Burma's largest ethnic minority, the Karens, of whom there are about seven million living in the jungles and hills of eastern Burma. I met her in December 2006, in a refugee camp in Thailand, the day before she and a group of more than a hundred Karens left for a new life in Canada.

The bright sunshine burned the banks of morning mist off the steep hillsides, as the people who were leaving wandered among the wooden shacks of the camp saying goodbye to friends, neighbours, aid workers, and teachers. Soon they would board a convoy of trucks to begin their long journey to the snowy streets of Winnipeg, Edmonton, and Vancouver.

Delia was eight years old when the Burmese army attacked her village. "I remember the shooting and the explosions," she says, "They attacked our village at night. We ran away into the jungle leaving everything behind."

Delia, her parents, and her small sister trekked through the jungle for weeks, and eventually made it to safety on the Thai side of the Salween River. She grew up, married, and had four children in refugee camps, never going outside the camp gates. The Thai authorities keep registered refugees as virtual prisoners, apparently fearing that easy registration, permission for work, or education outside the camps would make the life of a refugee so attractive that it would provoke an unmanageable flood across the border. Thailand only began allowing resettlement in third countries like Canada and Australia in 2006. Most of the hundreds of thousands of displaced Karens never make it to a safe haven in Thailand. Only a handful are offered new homes elsewhere.

For six decades, the Burmese regime has been gradually grinding down the ethnic insurrections. It has brought some groups under control by making deals with local warlords, and crushed others. It has never engaged in any serious dialogue with anyone who could claim to be truly representative of these minorities. The Karen army, divided since a dissident group defected to the government side, is now down to about four thousand soldiers, outnumbered a hundred-to-one by the vast Burmese army. As the Karens slowly lose the war, army attacks on villages intensify, as do rapes, killings, and forced labour.

My companions and I had snuck across the border into Burma with a team of backpack medics, young Karen exiles who head into the jungle for months at a time, carrying on their backs the only medical supplies that reach the Karen population. They treat vil-

lagers as they go. In one camp, a night's march from the Thai border, we found dozens of families who had just arrived. What had
happened to them is exactly what happened to Delia Sie more than
thirty years ago. "The troops came to the village and burned it
down. We all ran away," said Myalia Thoo. She had a baby in her
arms and three small children peeping out from behind her legs.
She had walked for ten days to reach the camp. Naw Saimon's family had been walking for two weeks after they were forced out of
their home. "They laid landmines all around the village. Some people stepped on them. We had to leave," she said.

Among the dozen or more ethnic armies that have reached an
accommodation with the generals in Rangoon is the United Wa
State Army (uwsa), which supervises the cultivation and transport of the world's second largest opium crop. In 2000, I went to
the Wa area, which straddles the border between Burma and
China's Yunnan Province, to see a demonstration of the regime's
drug-eradication program. It was a publicity stunt, like the annual
burning of symbolic quantities of drugs in Rangoon, which is
designed to draw attention away from the generals' complicity in
the drug trade.

Among the ethnic Chinese in this region are the descendants of
Ming dynasty loyalists who fled the rise of the Manchu Qing
dynasty in the seventeenth century, and the families of defeated
Guomindang soldiers who fled the rise of the Chinese Communist
Party in 1949. They have mingled with the Wa, once ferocious
headhunters.

As we watched local villagers, organized by uwsa, whack a
symbolic few hectares of poppy plants, I chatted with a leather-
faced old soldier named Bao You Yi. He and his brother Bao You
Xiang are two of the most powerful men in the drug trade. Bao
told me that the Wa were getting out of the drug business.
"Beginning more than a hundred years ago, we made our living

with the drug trade," he said. "But it has become quite harmful to us. The whole world sees drugs as the enemy, and now we see it that way, too."

A brand new pig farm and a vineyard were shown off as evidence that the Wa were going straight. "By 2005, there will be no more opium grown in the Wa area," said Bao You Yi. Of course, things did not quite turn out that way. In 2005, Burma produced 380 tonnes of opium, and had 40,000 hectares under poppy cultivation, an 11 percent increase over the previous year.

Like North Korea, Burma is uncontrovertibly in the hands of a rogue regime. The generals, fabulously wealthy from the drug trade, from gems, from the plunder of endangered forests, and from the sale of licences sold to unscrupulous businessmen and corporations, run a government that provides next to no services. An army almost half-a-million strong commits vile abuses with impunity, while political prisoners rot in jail. Both countries are run like criminal syndicates, and the two regimes' abuses are so extreme that reforms from within are no longer possible. And yet, there is no international strategy or will to bring about change.

———— · ————

IN THE SUMMER OF 2006, I telephoned Hu Jia, the young activist who three years earlier had helped me to report on the AIDS epidemic in Henan Province, to invite him to dinner. "I'm in hospital," he said, "but I can come out for a few hours. There will be some people with me. There are eight of them outside at the moment." In telling me this, he was not expecting me to entertain eight extra guests. Rather, he was warning me that he had an entourage of secret police following him, in case that might embarrass any of my other guests.

When Hu Jia arrived at the restaurant, with two carloads of men in plain clothes in tow, he looked about ten years older than when I had last seen him. Regular imprisonment and beatings were taking their toll. In 2003, when we had been working together on the AIDS program, I had been worried by his determination to speak out on even more controversial issues, such as the 1989 massacre or the Dalai Lama. "Your expertise and prominence on the AIDS issue give you a kind of umbrella," I suggested. "You can use it to say many critical things without offending the central government too much, but when you step out into areas like Tiananmen, things they regard as purely political, they are going to try to squash you."

"You know what my Internet name is, don't you?" Hu Jia responded.

"Freeborn."

"That's the way I live."

Hu Jia and his wife, Zeng Jinyan, were watched and followed constantly. He was regularly detained to prevent him from making such provocative gestures as laying flowers in Tiananmen Square. The couple documented their lives under surveillance, by posting pictures and videos of their watchers on their Internet blogs. Their integrity and courage attracted the attention of others who were struggling against the system. They became the centre of an informal network of lawyers, human-rights activists, and protestors, and their blogs became a vital source of information about abuses all over China. Meticulous accuracy made them better reporters than many of us who practise journalism as a profession.

"When I'm arrested, I demand to know what article of the constitution or what law I am supposed to have broken," Hu Jia says. "When the police don't have answers, I tell them, 'It is you who are breaking the law, not me.' I'm quite sorry for the ones who follow me. They are young guys in their twenties. I ask them why they don't do something useful with their lives."

The guests at my dinner in 2006 included several Western

journalists, but it was Hu Jia who reminded us that it was International Press Freedom Day, and proposed a toast. "I have to say that China has really come a long way on human rights, democracy, and freedom," he said. "Many of the things I do now would have been quite impossible, unthinkable, a few years ago."

Hu Jia reminds me of another Chinese political prisoner, Wei Jingsheng. He has the same single-minded conviction that he has found his moral compass, and will not deviate from it, whatever the cost. During a total of seventeen years in prison, Wei Jingsheng became the most famous, iconic prisoner-of-conscience in China. He began his protest in the late 1970s, when Deng Xiaoping was consolidating his position as supreme leader after the death of Mao Zedong. Deng allowed a brief flowering of free speech, expressed through the publishing of posters on a wall in western Beijing, which became known as the Democracy Wall. Deng was replacing Maoist dogma with the Four Modernizations: the rebuilding of China's industry, agriculture, national defence, and science and technology. Wei Jingsheng, yet another electrician-turned-dissident, went down to the wall one day from his job at the Beijing zoo and posted an essay called, "The Fifth Modernization," demanding democracy in China. He was soon arrested and spent the next fourteen years in prison.

I met him at his brother's home on the night he was released in September 1993. Wei had been let go a few days before the International Olympic Committee was to decide which city would host the 2000 Summer Games. He seemed shocked when I suggested that there was hope of a quid-pro-quo arrangement. "But that would be dirty politics!" he said, as if such a thing ought never to enter anyone's mind. "I don't see how releasing someone could have anything to do with it. The Olympics are supposed to be a sporting event, not a political one." I asked him if he thought his essay had been worth fourteen years in jail. "Certainly," he said. "I would do it again today, except that I would do it better than the twenty-eight-year-old Wei Jingsheng. Knowing what I know now, I have more experience and understanding. China still needs democracy, and the absence of democracy has been the main cause of many problems in the past."

A few days later, we learned that Sydney, Australia, got the 2000 Games instead of Beijing. Picking up his quarrel with Deng Xiaoping without missing a beat, Wei went on to behave as if he really was free, writing and saying what he wanted, until he was arrested again in 1994. After three more years in prison, he finally threw in the towel, and in 1997 he accepted an offer of permission to leave the country for medical treatment. Now he lives with the irrelevance of exile. In the United States, he can say whatever he wants to say, but no one is listening. The words wasted on the personal squabbles and historical bickering of exile politics say less than the stubborn silence of the prison cell.

Almost every single day I receive a self-promoting email from Wei Jingsheng's organization in the United States. They trumpet his great achievements, a prize awarded, or a call for action to put pressure on the Chinese government. I used to get regular emails from Hu Jia, too, but those stopped abruptly on December 27, 2007. Hu's emails sometimes consisted of witty and detailed records of the intrusions of the security apparatus into his life, and into the lives of his wife and their newborn daughter, but more often they were accurate and meticulous accounts of the persecution of others. The dangerous prominence he gained by refusing to shut up, made him a magnet for others who were willing to challenge the system, or who had become its victims. He passed on information to the world from an extraordinary network of Chinese dissidents, activists, lawyers, and persecuted individuals. His last email noted that he and his wife had been under "monitoring and control," a form of house arrest, for 222 days, and that the opening ceremony for the Beijing Olympics was 225 days away. The next morning, Hu was arrested again. His wife Zeng Jinyan's cellphone and computer were confiscated, and she and her daughter were "monitored" by an estimated fifty agents who had occupied the apartment above theirs. In March 2008, he was sentenced to three-and-a-half years in prison for "attempting to subvert the state's political power and socialist system." The prosecution quoted articles he had posted on the Internet, and interviews he had given to foreign journalists. Because they knew that Hu Jia would attract the attention of the thousands of international reporters about to descend on Beijing, the authorities locked him up to silence him during the Games.

The *jusqu'auboutiste* extreme defiance of people like Hu and Wei is so different from the survival strategy of practical compromise, compliance, or silence adopted by most Chinese that, when asked about well-known critics and opponents of the regime, many people tend to shake their heads and sigh, partly in admiration of their stubborn integrity and courage, partly to express doubts about their sanity. As Hu Jia himself noted in his toast to press freedom over dinner on May 3, 2006, Chinese people enjoy many freedoms today that were unimaginable twenty years ago. A young friend of mine, Wen Ling, is an example of those who would rather appreciate those freedoms than challenge the government by agitating for more. An artist in his late twenties, with a ready smile and a peering, quizzical expression that makes him look like a puzzled teddy bear, Wen Ling is constantly amused by life. He spends a lot of time out and about with his digital camera, looking for pictures to post on his popular photoblog.

"I take pictures of ordinary people's lives, what their homes are like, what they eat, what they do when they go out to play. Not life on the big, good-looking streets, just ordinary life on ordinary streets," he says. "I'm always looking out for something interesting. Things like: suddenly there's an argument, so I rush over to take a picture, then there's a traffic accident. Shoot that!" He belongs to a generation of youngsters who find more things possible, and more things permitted than ever before. They have little interest in politics. "We all keep our political opinions inside. We don't express them through action. I do my own thing, what I am interested in, making a living, getting on with my life. We're not like people in the 1980s who took certain actions. We are not very political."

Like most people in most places, most Chinese spend little time thinking about politics. They eat breakfast, lunch, and dinner, try to get on at work, hope they make the right choices for their children's education. Opinions in Beijing about the World Cup, the U.S. president, or what the rich and famous have been up to and with whom, are as diverse as opinions in Birmingham or Bogota.

Twenty years ago, when I was walking down a Chinese street for the first time, I was overwhelmed by the din of chatter I couldn't understand, and the clutter of signs, billboards, and slogans I couldn't read. I was instantly aware of being, not only speechless, but also illiterate, an infant unable to go shopping, order a meal, ask for directions, read a newspaper, or even pick the right bathroom without help, once I was outside the bubble of Western hotels and tourist spots. I used to think that, if only I could speak the language well, I would be able find out what is going on in this country, and understand what it all means. For centuries, foreign scholars, missionaries, traders, diplomats, and journalists have been swapping explanations of why China is the way it is, how to handle it, and where it is going. The fact is China is too big and complex, and the Chinese too numerous and various, for many of the explanations to make sense. The more I learn, the more I realize that every categorical pronouncement about China or the Chinese contains the seeds of its own contradiction. And the more I come to know China, the more I understand why every prediction will be wrong.

EPILOGUE

In September 2006, I exchanged full-time work on daily news for a contract to make documentaries. This now takes up about half of my time. The new arrangement gave me the freedom to do what occupies the other half: start a TV production company in Beijing to work on long-term projects documenting changes in China.

My partner in the company, Yan Yuping, believes in fastidious preparation and meticulous attention to detail. She observes my working style with the exasperated yet tolerant eye of a kindergarten teacher watching a class of grubby little boys rolling around in the dirt. She says my saving grace is that I have a good *ming*, a word that has no direct equivalent in English. It combines fate, destiny, and luck. For a journalist, it includes the essential knack of often being in the right place at the right time. Brandishing her *Webster's Collegiate Dictionary*, Yan Yuping says I should have called this book *Muddling Through* because the title describes my life perfectly: "achieving a degree of success without planning or effort."

This chronicle of my muddling through for almost three decades as a foreign correspondent is also an account of the persistent desire among human beings everywhere to have the freedom to live their lives as they please. Pointing out such a self-evident truth would seem trite and superfluous were it not so often overlooked by those in power. The frequent failure of outside intervention, and the over-riding importance of transparency and truthfulness in government are recurring themes. Just as I was finishing writing the book, during China's pre-Olympic spring of 2008, these themes began to resonate loudly. An outbreak of serious rioting in Lhasa, the capitol of Tibet, in mid-March was followed first by an international uproar over the Olympic torch relay, and then by a deadly earthquake in Sichuan Province in mid-May.

The history of Tibet's relationship with China over the past thousand years or so is much more complex than Western romantics would like to believe, and far less clear-cut than the account the Chinese authorities cling to. The arguments for and against Tibet's right to independence and China's assertion of sovereignty are made extensively and loudly elsewhere. I will not rehash them here. The issue in spring 2008 was not independence, as such, but the failure of half a century of Chinese governance in Tibet.

After the establishment of the People's Republic of China in 1949, Chinese troops entered Tibet in 1950. On March 10, 1959, Tibet's spiritual and temporal leader, the Dalai Lama, then twenty-three years old, fled into exile during a botched uprising against Chinese rule. On March 10, 2008, the forty-ninth anniversary of the Dalai Lama's flight from Tibet, there was a small, peaceful demonstration by monks in Lhasa. Four days later, tension around a monastery where some monks had been arrested led to a sudden explosion of violent riots in many parts of the city.

Mobs of Tibetans attacked businesses owned by ethnic Han Chinese and Hui Muslims, killing, looting, and burning. The police did not intervene for twenty-four hours. Finally, units of the People's Armed Police, and reportedly the army, were deployed in armoured vehicles to crush the riots. The uncertainty over the identity of the units involved arises from the fact that identifying marks on their uniforms and vehicles were removed or covered up. The purpose of concealment was for the government to avoid unwelcome parallels with the 1989 massacre of students in Beijing, and to avoid admission of the complete failure of normal policing. Soon the unrest spread to Tibetan areas of the Chinese provinces bordering Tibet — Sichuan, Yunnan, Gansu, and Qinghai — where demonstrations were also suppressed by armed force. The Chinese government said fewer than twenty people were killed, most of them ethnic Chinese victims of the mob. Tibetan exiles said more than two hundred died, mostly Tibetans killed by the security forces.

A couple of weeks after the riots, my colleagues and I were driving along the shore of Qinghai Lake. Unable to get to Tibet because it had been closed to foreign journalists, we had gone instead to Qinghai Province, which has a large Tibetan population. The Dalai Lama was born near the provincial capital Xining. In large parts of Qinghai, Tibet's unique culture and religion have as much a presence as in Tibet itself.

We had been in Qinghai for two days, staying one step ahead of the security forces who had been turning foreign journalists away, but we were having difficulty interviewing people in the middle of the crackdown. Driving along the lakeshore, we were trying to puzzle out what we could do to show viewers on the other side of the world something of how Tibetans felt when we spotted a strange figure bobbing up and down in the distance.

As we approached, we saw that it was a pilgrim making his way slowly along the deserted road. Stationary, he would rise on his toes like a ballet dancer and lift up his hands, palms together in a gesture of prayer above his head. Then he would fall gracefully to his hands and knees, lower his head, and slide himself forward on wooden paddles attached to his hands until he was fully prostrate, all the while quietly chanting prayers. Then he would bring his feet up to his hands, stand upright, and, having advanced one body length toward his destination, rise on his toes once again.

To be driving along an empty road and have exactly the person you need to interview pop up on the horizon is an example of good *ming*.

When the pilgrim saw us, he stopped. His face lit up with a wonderful smile when we told him we were making a program for Canadian television.

"Where are you going?" we asked.

"Lhasa," he beamed.

The Tibetan capital was two thousand kilometres down the road.

"When do think you will get there?"

"In three more years," he said. "I left home a year ago."

When he gets to Lhasa's Jokhang Temple, completing a pilgrimage devout Tibetan Buddhists make once in a lifetime, he will turn around and spend four more years returning to his home monastery in Qinghai. He told us he had heard from people along the way about the riots in Lhasa, but would not judge what had happened without seeing it for himself.

A government propaganda campaign, accusing the Dalai Lama of instigating the trouble to spoil the Olympic Games, was at its height. Officials denounced the Dalai Lama as "a wolf in monk's clothing" and "a monster with a human face and a beast's heart." Protestors were vilified as insurgents seeking Tibetan independence and trying to "split the motherland." Monasteries were under police control, and prayer had been replaced with "patriotic education" for the monks.

We asked the pilgrim the obvious question: What do Tibetans really want?

"I hope the Dalai Lama will be able to come back to China. That's what I hope," he said, still beaming from ear to ear. "I want there to be peace everywhere. Tell everyone in Canada that all Tibetans hope that the Dalai Lama will come back to China."

Later that day, as we stopped at a toll booth on the way back to town, our car was surrounded by ten policemen. We were ordered out and held for three hours before we could negotiate our release with the help of the Foreign Ministry in Beijing. Under the rules covering foreign journalists — introduced to comply with International Olympic Committee standards — we had broken no law, so we were able to resist demands for our videotapes. But our reporting trip was nevertheless finished. Having been spotted and identified, we would now be relentlessly followed, and anyone we tried to talk to would be intimidated into silence.

Faced with the rioting in Lhasa, the Chinese government missed a golden opportunity to try out the policy of honesty and openness it had promised when it signed up for the Olympic Games. It reverted instead to its traditional strategies: keeping foreigners out, giving the security forces full reign, cracking down on dissent, and launching a hysterical propaganda campaign. As a result, there were competing narratives of what had occurred.

With no reporters on the ground, Western media generally underplayed the fact that Tibetans had committed an ugly pogrom against Han Chinese and Hui Muslims in Lhasa, and overplayed the image of monks being beaten by police, even misidentifying photos from protests in Nepal and India as having been taken in Tibet.

Chinese reports, including much of the coverage in the Chinese-language press outside China, underplayed the genuine grievances nurtured by Tibetans over being gradually outnumbered in their own capital by Han and Hui immigrants during half a century of clumsy Chinese rule. The Chinese media focus was entirely on the murdered Chinese and the non-existent plot by the Dalai Lama to promote independence by sabotaging the Olympics. Any other version of events was portrayed as a grievous insult to the dignity of Chinese people everywhere.

By the time the Olympic torch left Beijing on its world tour, guarded by a phalanx of sinister goons in blue tracksuits, international public opinion was primed for sympathy with the protestors, who had been planning for years to use Olympic events to draw attention to Tibet. Meanwhile, Chinese opinion around the world was primed for efforts to protect the "sacred flame," not as a symbol of the games or of the Chinese government, but as representing the racial and cultural pride of all Chinese.

Shrill statements from Chinese government officials and ambassadors praised the mobs of Chinese students who "defended the flame" by attacking protestors in South Korea, Australia, and elsewhere, and whipped up a vicious cyber-mob on the Chinese-language Internet. There was a campaign of death threats against Western reporters, and Chinese bulletin boards and chat rooms, normally swept clean of "forbidden speech," tolerated countless calls for violent attacks on the few users who committed "treason" by suggesting that the failure of Chinese governance in Tibet demanded a review of China's Tibet policy. Jin Jing, the Paralympic fencer who became a national heroine when she shielded the torch against protestors in Paris, was vilified after she voiced doubts about the campaign to boycott the French supermarket Carrefour. When Grace Wang, a Duke University student in the United States, tried to mediate between groups of Tibetan and Chinese fellow-students, the Internet mob called for her to be raped and murdered, and her parents had to leave home after their address was posted on the net.

The phenomenon of mob hysteria in Chinese cyberspace is not new. I noticed it in 2006, when a student whose handle was *bronze mustache* became an Internet celebrity after a user named *freezing blade* started an "Internet hunt" for him because of compromising email correspondence he had discovered between *bronze mustache* and his (*freezing blade*'s) wife, *quiet moon*. Hundreds of thousands of people denounced *bronze mustache* until the student was publicly identified and hounded out of his university. Similar campaigns, with violent language far out of proportion to the supposed offence, have become a particular feature of the Chinese Internet. The phenomenon is partly explained by how easy it is to post the most outrageous anonymous opinion online, compared with the relative lack of opportunity for free expression in the real world in China. But some Chinese commentators also find an unpleasant echo of the mass "struggle sessions" of the Cultural Revolution.

What was new in the Internet campaigns that followed the riots in Lhasa was that the government encouraged the "cybernationalist" movement, and called for more "reasonable" patriotic expression only after realizing the damage that was being done to the image China had been projecting of a great and peaceful nation gracefully taking its rightful place in the world after a long decline.

Aware that international pressure on the Tibet issue would not subside at least until after the Olympics, the Chinese government defused some criticism by re-opening talks with representatives of the Dalai Lama, without giving any public sign that it was willing to examine new ways of thinking about attitudes and policies which have produced such festering resentment. Nor was there any sign of appreciation that even if Tibet is not another country, Tibetans *are* another people, and that they could perhaps feel much the same self-righteous indignation over heavy-handed Chinese governance that the Chinese felt over foreign interlopers in the nineteenth and twentieth centuries, and still feel today over foreign pressure to change the way they do things.

The storm over Tibet was abating somewhat when the earthquake struck on May 12. Whereas the Tibet crisis brought out the worst in the Chinese government, the earthquake brought out the best — at first. The response was immediate, responsible, and remarkably open. The prime minister was on a plane to the earthquake zone within a couple of hours. Chinese television began marathon broadcasts, and foreign reporters were welcomed rather than turned away.

The comparison with Burma, which had been struck by a deadly cyclone just a few days before, was striking. The Burmese generals closed their borders, allowed in a trickle of material aid, which soldiers grabbed at Rangoon airport, and preferred to watch tens of thousands die than allow their prison of a country to be contaminated by the presence of foreign aid workers. Only a few years ago, China would have done the same. Instead, the Chinese People's Liberation Army organized a creditable early relief effort, and outside medical and rescue experts were welcomed in with little fuss or fanfare.

On the first day of the earthquake, Premier Wen Jiabao was seen shedding tears over children trapped under the ruins of their school, and calling out to them, "This is Grandpa Wen Jiabao. The government is coming to help you!" Even the television coverage seemed fresh and enterprising. Why, one Chinese reporter wondered at a government briefing, had so many schools collapsed when government buildings were safe and sound?

Internet public opinion swung behind earthquake relief, and turned on the organizers of the torch relay who had carried on as if nothing had happened, celebrating the great and glorious progress of the "sacred flame" through Fujian Province while people were dying in Sichuan. There was instant uproar over their lack of humanity. Chastened, the Olympic organizers turned each leg of the relay into a fundraising run, starting with a silent homage to earthquake victims.

It was a brief glimpse of what a more open China might be like, but it was short-lived. By day two the television coverage began to take on a new tone dictated by the propaganda department. There was round-the-clock coverage of tireless leaders directing heroic soldiers, and an endless series of interviews with survivors accepting aid, saying, "Thank you government! Thank you government!" There was no more mention of the ten thousand children who had lost their lives in the collapse of shoddy school buildings. News organizations were ordered not to investigate the national disgrace of corruption, embezzlement, and incompetence among building firms and government officials responsible for school construction and safety standards. Distraught parents holding vigils demanding the truth were dragged away by police.

By the time three days of national mourning were declared one week after the earthquake, a vast patriotic propaganda campaign was in full swing. Three minutes of silence were followed by a flag-waving, fist-pumping demonstration in Tiananmen Square, complete with the slogan that would greet Chinese athletes at the Games in August: "*Zhongguo Jia You!*" "Go, China, Go!"

Once again, the Communist Party threw away an opportunity for national dignity, honesty, and openness, offering instead a cover-up and the cheap chauvinism of the football crowd.

The Chinese government, so confident and mature when it comes to technical, practical challenges — from running a central bank to the first response to a gigantic natural disaster — can be as insecure and defensive as any adolescent when it comes to dealing with people, their opinions, and possible criticism of its own short-comings. The Communist Party has only a few years' experience trying to run a modern country. The transition from Marx to the market is bringing dramatic social changes, which need a new approach. Instead, obsessed with stability, the government resorts to rigid authoritarianism by covering up unpalatable truths and quashing dissent and discontent with force. It's a strategy that makes China and its government less stable, rather than more so. In earthquake zones, it is the structures which combine integrity, strength, and flexibility that survive.

BEIJING, CHINA

JUNE 4, 2008

ACKNOWLEDGEMENTS

Broadcast journalism is a team effort, but praise and awards for work well done are usually directed toward just one member of the team — the wrong one. In television, pictures are paramount, and the most important contributor to any television project is not the reporter who appears on the screen and writes and narrates the script, but the person behind the camera. In a different kind of memoir I would have had a thousand anecdotes to tell about the people who have shared my life on the road, and their part in covering the events described in this book. This time, I felt it better for them to remain in the background. Nevertheless, all the awards and the praise given to me for work in television truly belong to the calm craftsmen who consistently produced wonderful images in the most trying and dangerous conditions. They are also great friends and travelling companions. I offer my thanks and whole-hearted admiration to Philippe Billard, Andrew Clark, Tim Deagle, Charles Dubois, Louis de Guise, Rick Dobrucki, Brian Kelly, Mark Laban, Glen Kugelstadt, Pascal Leblond, Sat Nandlall, Peter Rosenfeld, Ian Wilson, and Peter Zim.

In television, the awards and praise should be shared by the editors. Like magicians, the greatest expression of their art is to render their skill invisible. They add pace, rhythm, suspense, and coherence to the work of others. It has been a pleasure working with Colin Dean, Kathy Durnin, Daniel Morin, Yves Pelletier, and Mary Wong.

Producers are the tour managers, hoteliers, logisticians, talent-bookers, editorial referees, and psychotherapists of the road. I cherish my memories of travels with Marie-Eve Bedard, Wyvina Belmonte, Tony Burman, Edith Champagne, David Clifton, Don Dixon, Valma Glenn, M. P. Nunan, Kas Roussy, Halina St-James, Corinne Seminoff, Yan Yuping, and Zhang Yongning.

Finally, my thanks to Daniel Boily, Jeff Brown, Brien Christie, Anne Hallerman, Tim Hardinge, Danielle Levasseur, and Bruno Tremblay for their patience, forbearance, and wisdom as assignment editors.

My dear friends and colleagues Fergal Keane and Yan Yuping read this book in manuscript and offered many helpful suggestions. I should have followed them all.

For the reader's interest, translations of Matteo Ricci's writings on pages 164, 165, and 174 were quoted from *China: A New History* by John King Fairbank and Merle Goldman and *The Memory Palace of Matteo Ricci* by Jonathan Spence.

INDEX

ABOUT THE AUTHOR

A foreign correspondent since 1980, PATRICK BROWN has reported on China since 1989. He has also covered revolutions, elections, wars, and disasters throughout Europe, the Middle East, and Asia. His radio and television reports in English and French have won several awards. Born in Birmingham, England, and educated at Downing College, Cambridge, he lived and worked in Montreal throughout the 1970s. He lives in Beijing.